Transformational Discipleship

Transformational Discipleship

how people really grow

ERIC GEIGER ●
MICHAEL KELLEY ●
PHILIP NATION ●

B&H
PUBLISHING GROUP
Nashville, Tennessee

978-1-4336-7854-7

Published by B&H Publishing Group
Nashville, Tennessee

Dewey Decimal Classification: 248.84
Subject Heading: DISCIPLESHIP \ CHRISTIAN LIFE \
SPIRITUAL LIFE

1 2 3 4 5 6 7 8 9 10 • 17 16 15 14 13 12

CONTENTS

DEDICATION

FROM ERIC

For my daughter Evie, full of life:

You brighten every room and constantly bring joy to your daddy.

In memory of two friends and pastors, Bill Carp and Michael Smith. When I was in a teachable posture as a nineteen-year-old youth pastor, Michael was a leader who supplied wisdom and direction. When I was new in Miami and feeling vulnerable, Bill, who served at the Vineyard, was a leader who provided godly friendship and encouragement.

FROM MICHAEL

For the people of Grace Community Church:

It continues to be my great joy to see how the gospel is continually preached and lived out in our midst.

FROM PHILIP

For my sons, Andrew and Chris:

My hope is that you will live wild adventures for our great King.

INTRODUCTION

by Ed Stetzer and Thom Rainer

"WE WANT TO GO DEEPER."

If you've been involved in church leadership for very long, that's a phrase you've probably heard before. Christians far and wide are craving to "go deeper." Fair enough, but the problem comes in knowing exactly what that means. Does it mean deeper in knowledge? Does it mean deeper in intimacy? In love? This is when the issue becomes more complicated.

Nevertheless, the sentiment is valid: Christians want to grow in their faith. Really grow. This is not only an encouraging and worthwhile desire but a biblical one as well. One of the most beautiful images of this kind of growth comes straight from the description of the man who trusts in the Lord from Jeremiah 17:7–8: "The man who trusts in the LORD, whose confidence indeed is the LORD, is blessed. He will be like a tree planted by water: it sends its roots out toward a stream, it doesn't fear when heat comes, and its foliage remains green. It will not worry in a year of drought or cease producing fruit."

How is it, even during times of great drought, that such a tree never ceases to bear fruit? It's because the roots of that tree have grown deep.

Several years ago we wrote the book *Transformational Church*. Based on one of the largest research projects ever completed on church health, it offered a message of hope for the church. Far from the pessimism that abounds regarding the state of the church in many circles, through extensive research we found that many churches are flourishing. People are growing, and entire communities are being transformed because of believers that care more about God's mission than the survival of traditions.

The church is alive and well, and certain tendencies mark congregations that have a profound, transformational impact. Among the conclusions from that project was this simple but powerful one: God shapes congregations through the shaping of individual lives. Further, this shaping of individuals doesn't just happen; it's through intentional effort on the part of both leaders and church members.

While most every leader knows this is true, much confusion still abounds about how people really grow. The book you hold in your hands is meant to be a helpful tool in describing that process. It's the next step in discovering how God shapes and forms believers into the kind of people described in Jeremiah 17.

What you'll find in this book isn't a prescriptive process. It isn't a magic formula or a church mantra to be echoed. Instead, it's the result of extensive research with churches and individuals who have answered the call of Jesus to make disciples. It's not only the compilation of their wisdom and stories but also a guide for leaders to practice the kind of intentional efforts it will take in order to create not a program but an entire culture in which people will grow.

And they will grow. It's not because of what you read in this book. Neither is it because of any program that might be instituted. Rather, it's because disciples are being made in the same way they've always been made—by the power of the Holy Spirit working through the church. It is when people of God engage in the mission of God through the Spirit of God.

The three authors who have taken on the task of writing this book are men we know and trust. Eric, Michael, and Philip love Christ and serve His church. Each has a unique perspective because of their individual journeys of discipleship. But they agree that the church can and must do better. So, with faithfulness to the Scriptures and data from the most recent research about spiritual development, they have written *Transformational Discipleship*.

Our great hope is that as you read, you will begin to see both the simplicity and the complexity of the great task before us. We hope you will be renewed in your vision to see people grow in Christ, and you will find new hope for all God is doing in and through His people.

1
Deficient Discipleship

Christianity without the living Christ
is inevitably Christianity without discipleship,
and Christianity without discipleship is always
Christianity without Christ.
—Dietrich Bonhoeffer[1]

IN THE LEADER'S FINAL HOURS, he was almost completely alone. He faced death without the company of those who swore their allegiance. Most of his trusted and closest friends deserted him. Some fled and painfully betrayed him. The world scorned him.

But not this disciple.

This disciple would remain faithful to death, following his leader to the grave. His mind was fully committed, his will set on his leader's agenda, and his heart thrilled by the intimacy of the relationship with his teacher. He was in awe of his king, humbled to be included in the inner circle. This disciple wrote of an early encounter with his leader:

Great joy. He greets me like an old friend. And looks after me. How I love him! Then he speaks. How small I am.[2]

Later the disciple penned these words about his leader's teaching and influence:

When he speaks, all resistance breaks down before the magical effect of his words. One can only be his friend or his enemy. He divides the hot from the cold. But lukewarmness he spits out of his mouth.[3]

The disciple is famous, just as his leader.

Before his death he said of himself and his leader, "We shall go down in history as the greatest statesmen of all time, or the greatest criminals."

The disciple's name was Joseph Goebbels, and he was a disciple of his Fuhrer (his leader), Adolph Hitler. While others deserted Hitler, Goebbels spent his last days alongside him in Hitler's secure bunker. When Hitler committed suicide, Goebbels and his wife followed closely behind after killing their six children. Goebbels was correct; they are known as the greatest criminals in history. The atrocities they committed against humanity are disgusting. Their plan to eliminate the Jewish people was twisted and evil.

Goebbels was a true disciple of Hitler, a follower, a student. He trusted and emulated his leader. He was discipled, but his heart was obviously never transformed. He died a wicked man with a depraved heart of stone.

Not all discipleship is transformational.

Chris Farley is still regarded as one of the funniest comedians of our generation. From his sketches on *Saturday Night Live* to the movies he starred in, Farley was a success in the entertainment business.

Chris Farley was impacted by the example and influence of another famous comedian: John Belushi. In a real sense Farley was a disciple of Belushi. Farley famously admitted, "I wanted to be like him in every way." John Belushi moved from the comedy troupe, Second City, in Chicago to *Saturday Night Live* to starring in movies. Farley followed the same career path.

Farley's emulation did not stop there. Both Belushi and Farley struggled with obesity and had a reputation for wild living. Sadly Belushi died of a drug overdose when he was only thirty-three years old. And years later, after a night of partying, Chris Farley was found dead in his apartment from a drug overdose. He was thirty-three years old. While his mentor impacted his aspirations and his behavior, his mentor never transformed his heart.

Not all discipleship is transformational.

Nontransformational Discipleship

Every person who has ever lived is a disciple. Every person in your church, neighborhood, and community is a disciple. In the New Testament the word for *disciple* is the Greek word *math-etes*, which can also be translated *pupil* or *apprentice*. *Disciple* simply means "learner or student." Therefore, everyone everywhere is a disciple of someone. Or something.

> *Every person who has ever lived is a disciple.*

Jesus warns us to be careful whom we follow because, as happened with Goebbels and Farley, we will become like our leader. In Luke 6, Jesus gathered a large crowd to Himself and challenged the people to consider carefully who they would learn from, who they would follow. They had many teachers to choose from, and

Jesus used a brief parable to show the people the seriousness of the choice.

> He also told them a parable: "Can the blind guide the blind? Won't they both fall into a pit? A disciple is not above his teacher, but everyone who is fully trained will be like his teacher." (Luke 6:39–40)

Jesus was speaking among a plethora of religious teachers who led people away from the grace of God. To the crowd Christ was saying, "Follow the wrong leader, and he will lead you into a pit." We become like the teacher we admire, so be careful.

When Jesus entered our world, He intentionally stepped into a Jewish discipleship paradigm filled with rabbis and disciples. There were numerous traveling rabbis in Jesus' culture, but their discipleship was not transformational. The learners were impacted by the knowledge and skills they learned, but their hearts were never transformed. Everyone is a disciple, but not everyone is transformed.

Only one Leader brings transformation to His disciples.

Discipleship apart from Jesus is nontransformational. It may bring changes, but it essentially leaves you in the same spiritual state as it found you. The discipleship may provide education, improve behavior, increase happiness, add value, or make the disciple more skilled at a craft. But these are just *changes*. It's the reskinning of the same thing on the inside.

Surely we can all relate to what it means to be discipled by culture. If not, just take a look at a picture of yourself from fifteen or twenty years ago. Those clothes? That hairstyle? The music you were listening to? Looking back, you can't believe you thought any of those things were acceptable, much less cool. What's worse, you can't imagine that you—*you*—would ever wear or listen to it. But the *you* of middle or high school was absolutely convinced not only that your clothes or music was cool but that they were what you really wanted. Discipleship apart from Jesus may be many things, but it is not transformational. Jesus is the only Rabbi who has the power to transform lives.

Jesus isn't just a passing fad, soon to be replaced by another right around the corner. If you believe what the Bible says, Jesus doesn't change people's clothes; He changes the very fabric of people's being. He brings light to darkness. He brings death to life. He brings new to the old. The transformation Jesus offers is radically different from simply being conformed to the world.

One of the clearest statements in the New Testament that makes this distinction is in the well-worn verses of Romans 12:1–2.

> Therefore, brothers, by the mercies of God, I urge you
> to present your bodies as a living sacrifice, holy and
> pleasing to God; this is your spiritual worship. Do not
> be conformed to this age, but be transformed by the
> renewing of your mind, so that you may discern what is
> the good, pleasing, and perfect will of God.

The difference is vitally important. The world seeks, through a million marketing messages every day, to conform our thinking to its standards. Most of us are more influenced by these messages than we realize. We will, in fact, either be conformed or transformed. Jesus isn't merely interested in conforming—changing the appearance and behavior of people. He's interested in transformation. Transformation is more than a surface-level alteration; it's actually becoming something else entirely.

Transformation only comes through the discipleship that is centered on Jesus.

Not all discipleship is transformational, but transformation only comes through the discipleship that is centered on Jesus.

Discipleship Deficiency

Since Christ-centered discipleship results in transformation, we can confidently assert that most churches are deficient in discipleship. This is a scathing claim as our entire mission as believers and churches is to "make disciples." After His death and resurrection, Jesus was clear in His command to His first disciples:

> Go, therefore, and make disciples of all nations, baptizing them in the name of the Father and of the Son and of the Holy Spirit, teaching them to observe everything I have commanded you. And remember, I am with you always, to the end of the age. (Matt. 28:19–20)

The reason Jesus left His disciples on the planet was to make other disciples. The fundamental reason your church exists is to make disciples of Jesus.

To the church at Colossae, the apostle Paul wrote a defining statement about his ministry to the church:

> I have become its [the church's] servant, according to God's administration that was given to me for you, to make God's message fully known, the mystery hidden for ages and generations but now revealed to His saints. God wanted to make known to those among the Gentiles the glorious wealth of this mystery, which is Christ in you, the hope of glory. We proclaim Him, warning and teaching everyone with all wisdom, so that we may present everyone mature in Christ. I labor for this,

striving with His strength that works powerfully in me.
(Col. 1:25–29)

The apostle Paul labored with the energy of Christ to present everyone mature and transformed in Christ. Because Paul was convinced that transformation only comes through Christ, he labored to make disciples of Jesus and not of himself.

For a church to be deficient in discipleship is to be deficient in its fundamental reason for existence. If any organization is careless in its core reason for existence, it doesn't matter if the organization excels at other things.

If Apple is deficient in designing computers, it doesn't matter if they excel in outfitting and decorating their stores. If Starbucks is deficient in coffee, mastering the art of creating loyal employees means nothing. To be deficient in your core reason for existence is always unacceptable.

We have learned to do many things as church leaders and members.

We build buildings.

We design programs.

We staff our churches.

We put on events.

We rally people around new initiatives.

And as our churches grow, we become increasingly proficient in a myriad of other things from branding to facility management. But are we making disciples? Have we become proficient in many things while simultaneously becoming deficient in the one thing that matters most?

When the apostle Paul felt compelled to defend his ministry, he did not point to his savvy leadership, the size of this team, the creativity or innovation in his ministry, his speaking ability, or even the number of mission trips he was leading. He simply pointed to the transformation in people's lives.

> Are we beginning to commend ourselves again? Or do we need, like some, letters of recommendation to you or from you? You yourselves are our letter, written on our hearts, recognized and read by everyone. It is clear that you are Christ's letter, produced by us, not written with ink but with the Spirit of the living God—not on stone tablets but on tablets that are hearts of flesh. (2 Cor. 3:1–3)

Paul essentially says: "I don't need a resume that outlines my effectiveness as a disciple-maker. Look at the transformed lives because those lives are the resume. But please understand, I did not write the resume. Christ did. And when He wrote it, He wrote it on the hearts of people." Transformation is the bottom-line result of true discipleship.

Looking into the Church

So how can we—the church—know whether or not transformational discipleship is occurring? We decided to study the issue. In 2008, LifeWay Research surveyed seven thousand churches to discover the principles involved with congregational health and published their findings in the book *Transformational Church*. The findings from that research project have helped many churches find renewal and their place in God's mission. The "Transformational Church Assessment Tool" (TCAT) crafted from the study findings is being used by churches in urban, suburban, rural, domestic, and international locations to rediscover who God intends them to be.

In 2010, LifeWay Research embarked on another ambitious research project: to survey believers about their spiritual lives and level of maturity. Building on the Transformational Church survey and the research behind the book *The Shape of Faith to Come* by Brad Waggoner, we looked into the major areas of life where spiritual maturity takes place.

The research was done in three phases. First, a qualitative survey of experts in the field of discipleship was completed. Members of the research team did interviews with recognized experts including pastors, professors, and church leaders from a variety of backgrounds. Here is the list of experts we spoke to:

- Jerry Acosta—evangelism coordinator with the Venezuelan National Baptist Convention
- Francisco Aular—pastor in Canada and founder of the Latin American Baptist Discipleship Movement
- Henry Blackaby—president of Blackaby Ministries and author of *Experiencing God*
- Luis "Gary" Cesar—senior pastor of First Baptist Church Satelite
- Marigene Chamberlain—professor at Samford University and former member of General Board of Discipleship, The United Methodist Church
- Neil Cole—founder and director of Church Multiplication Associates
- Robert Coleman—author of *Master Plan of Discipleship*
- Hector Hugo Arias Contreras—leader at the Chilean Baptist Convention
- Earl Creps—professor of leadership and spiritual renewal at Assemblies of God Theological Seminary and author of *Off-Road Disciplines*
- Edgard Castano Diaz—senior pastor of Central Baptist Church, Bogota, Columbia, and former president of the Colombian Evangelical Council

- Jon Ferguson—teaching pastor, Community Christian Church
- Angel Mena Garcia—pastor and denominational leader with the Assemblies of God in Panama
- Alton Garrision—assistant general superintendent, Assemblies of God
- Billie Hanks—founder of Operation Multiplication
- Alan Hirsch—founder of Forge
- T. W. Hunt—author of *The Mind of Christ* and *The Doctrine of Prayer*
- Mary Kassian—professor at The Southern Baptist Theological Seminary and author of *In My Father's House*
- Larry Lee—executive secretary of Youth and Leadership Development of National Evangelical Christian Fellowship Malaysia
- Aubrey Malphurs—founder of The Malphurs Group, professor at Dallas Theological Seminary, and author of *Advanced Strategic Planning* and *Strategic Disciple Making*
- Robertson McQuilkin—president emirtus of Columbia International University
- Jaime Riquelme Miranda—pastor and leader of the Chilean Ministers Alliance
- Alexander Montero—director of Venezuelan National Baptist Convention
- Steve Murrell—founding pastor of Victory Fellowship, Manila
- Waldemar Morales Roca—director of Guatemala Baptist Seminary
- Leonard Sweet—professor at Drew University and author of *The Gospel According to Starbucks*
- Natan Velazquez—pastor of Emmanuel Baptist Church, Caracas, Venezuela

- Victor Villanueva—leader at the Mexico National Baptist Convention and professor at Yucatan Autonomous University
- Don Whitney—professor of biblical spirituality at The Southern Baptist Theological Seminary and author of *Spiritual Disciplines for the Christian Life*

As you can see, it is a diverse lineup. From these experts in the field of discipleship, the research team gained a better understanding of what is taking place in the church both domestically and in other countries (specifically in the Hispanic context).

After the expert interview phase, the research team conducted a survey of one thousand Protestant pastors in the United States. The survey discovered the type of discipleship ministries being used in churches and the satisfaction level they have with them. The survey revealed a great deal of paradoxes occurring between pastors' hope that people are maturing and the level of satisfaction they have that believers truly are maturing.

Finally, LifeWay Research did a survey of four thousand Protestants in North America. Of that number, approximately eleven hundred were in Canada. The survey was done in three languages: English, Spanish, and French. The survey was built on research from the Spiritual Formation Inventory (SFI) that came from Waggoner's previous research. In the SFI research, seven domains of the Christian life were identified that lead to spiritual health in a believer. The team built on the seven domains and added factors based on the expert interviews. Ultimately the research revealed an eighth domain that points to spiritual health. We will refer to these as attributes of discipleship.

Throughout the upcoming chapters, we will refer to statistics from the eight attributes. Though this is not a statistically heavy book, research findings will be present throughout. We believe that the Bible is sufficient for equipping us to grow in our faith. We also believe that seeking to understand what Christ is doing in His people in the current day is a wise course of action.

So, when you see a statistic quoted, don't pass by too quickly; but, as we have done, seek to learn from what God is doing in our brothers and sisters in the faith. We all need to learn what practices and attitudes will most effectively be used by Christ to transform us into His likeness.

Sadly, we can make this bold diagnosis based on the far-reaching and sobering research:

> There is a discipleship deficiency in most churches
> resulting in a lack of transformation.

In the survey of one thousand Protestant pastors regarding the status of discipleship in their churches, only 47 percent agree with the statement: "I am satisfied with the state of discipleship and spiritual formation in our local church." Though the study revealed that most churches have an intention of discipleship, most leaders are not satisfied with the effectiveness of their ministry.

When the same group of pastors was asked about the statement, "We are consistently hearing reports of changed lives at our church," they gave a 49 percent response to "strongly agree" and 41 percent to "somewhat agree" categories. At best, we have some paradoxes to deal with from church leaders. They know lives are being changed at some level but not with consistency from the ministries of the church. The sad reality is that the daily lives, aspirations, and desires of many people in our churches mirror those who do not claim to know Christ.

Facing the Discipleship Reality

We have a transformation problem.

But we have known that, and you know it too. So instead of conducting a research project primarily aimed at further exposing the lack of transformational discipleship in most churches, we took another angle. The team of researchers and leaders from LifeWay Research sought to uncover what kind of discipleship is truly transformational. We dug into the lives of the people in churches where changed lives are more the norm than the exception. The research also included personal interviews with discipleship experts, godly leaders who have poured their lives into seeing transformation in people. Then, using their insights and previous research, we conducted an in-depth survey with four thousand believers in North America (using English, Spanish, and French surveys). The results have led us to understand better what is happening among God's people and to have hope for the possibility of transformational discipleship.

> *We have a transformation problem.*

From the research we developed a framework for transformational discipleship, which we will present in chapter 3 and unpack throughout the book. But we need to lay a discipleship foundation first.

Discipleship is a word that is often hijacked and haphazardly tossed around to describe a multitude of things. And because it has become such a nebulous term, people launch complaints about a ministry described as "discipleship" that may not have the slightest resemblance to what is possible in delivering transformation to people.

ficiency flows from a faulty understanding of
church or an individual has an inaccurate view
, the resulting impact is horrifyingly huge. We have
o common yet flawed views that unfortunately impact
a church's likelihood to make disciples that are transformed: equating information with discipleship and viewing discipleship merely as behavioral modification. Discipleship is much more than information and much deeper than behavioral modification.

More than Information

Many churches equate discipleship with knowledge. If you are a church leader with this predisposition, you believe the solution to a discipleship deficiency is more classroom time. Churches who view discipleship as information transfer seek to stuff as much biblical knowledge into as many people as quickly as they possibly can. It sounds noble, but the essence of discipleship is transformational not informational.

Jesus commanded, "Go . . . and make disciples . . . teaching them to *observe* everything I have commanded" (Matt. 28:19–20). Jesus did not merely ask us to teach everything He commanded. He asked us to teach people to obey everything He commanded, and the difference is mammoth. The end result of discipleship is not merely the *knowledge of* all Jesus commanded but the *obedience to* all Jesus commanded.

The difference can be easily illustrated through the life of Judas Iscariot, who should have been the poster child for discipleship. Judas was filled with information about Jesus, but he was never truly transformed by Jesus. In Matthew 26, Judas admits that he has never been transformed. Jesus and the disciples gathered for the Passover meal where Jesus would take the elements and give them new meaning that would point to His death and the forgiveness of sins.

> When evening came, He was reclining at the table with the Twelve. While they were eating, He said, "I assure you: One of you will betray Me." Deeply distressed, each one began to say to Him, "Surely not I, Lord?" He replied, "The one who dipped his hand with Me in the bowl—he will betray Me. The Son of Man will go just as it is written about Him, but woe to that man by whom the Son of Man is betrayed! It would have been better for that man if he had not been born." Then Judas, His betrayer, replied, "Surely not I, Rabbi?" "You have said it," He told him. (Matt. 26:20–26)

Jesus tells Judas, "You have said it. You have just admitted that you're the one who will betray me, the one who is not truly my disciple."

What did Judas say?

Notice the language in the passage. The other eleven disciples respond to Jesus' statement that a betrayer is among them with, "Surely not I, *Lord*?" But Judas responds differently, "Surely not I, *Rabbi*?"

The other disciples had surrendered their lives to Jesus. He was their Lord. To Judas, Jesus was a Rabbi he respected, spent time with, and learned from, but Jesus was not the Lord of his life. Judas never surrendered his will to Jesus. He was informed but never transformed.

From Judas we learn that knowledge about Christ alone does not result in true discipleship. Judas knew all about Jesus. He heard every sermon Jesus preached. He personally saw Jesus confront the religious and welcome sinners. Judas saw Jesus put light into the eyes of blind men, tell paralyzed men to pick up their mats and walk, raise the dead, heal lepers, and cast out demons. He saw firsthand the power and love of God perfectly displayed in Jesus. He knew everything about Christ, but he was not transformed.

James 2:19 says, "You believe that God is one; you do well. The demons also believe—and they shudder." If information about Jesus equals discipleship, the demons would be disciples. Judas respected Jesus as Rabbi but never trusted Him as Lord. Judas learned from Jesus' teaching but never allowed Jesus' teaching to transform him. And Jesus would not be Judas's Savior because He was not Judas's Lord. A. W. Tozer wrote:

> I warn you—you will not get help from Him in that way for the Lord will not save those whom He cannot command! He will not divide His offices. You cannot believe on a half-Christ. We take Him for what He is— the anointed Savior and Lord who is King of kings and Lord of lords! He would not be who He is if He saved us and called us and chose us without the understanding that He can also guide and control our lives.[4]

Churches that are transformational in discipleship help people encounter Jesus as Lord and not merely as Rabbi.

The Curse of Knowledge

Jesus never equated knowledge with discipleship. In fact, His most blistering rebukes were directed at groups of people who were filled with knowledge about Him. One of the most stunning is found in Matthew 11.

> Then He proceeded to denounce the towns where most of His miracles were done, because they did not repent:

"Woe to you, Chorazin! Woe to you, Bethsaida! For if the miracles that were done in you had been done in Tyre and Sidon, they would have repented in sackcloth and ashes long ago! But I tell you, it will be more tolerable for Tyre and Sidon on the day of judgment than for you." (Matt. 11:20–22)

The cities of Chorazin and Bethsaida were geographically close to each other. In fact, they along with Capernaum, where Jesus lived during His ministry, formed a small triangle. Scholars refer to that as the "evangelical triangle," the region where Jesus performed the majority of His miracles, selected His

> *Jesus never equated knowledge with discipleship.*

first disciples, and preached His greatest sermons. The evangelical triangle is like an ancient version of our modern-day Bible Belt, where churches are on every corner and the vast majority of people would claim to be Christian simply because they were born into a Christian family, received an attendance sticker at Vacation Bible School, or helped with some type of annual Christmas play with live animals.

The people in this region viewed themselves as religiously superior to the rest of the world. After all, they were Israel, the ones who were chosen by God, had received the law, and had enjoyed a great spiritual heritage and pedigree.

Jesus rocks their world by telling them that Tyre and Sidon would have repented in sackcloth and ashes if they had observed the same miracles. Sackcloth and ashes were symbols of extreme brokenness before God and were used to mark public repentance. Jesus shocks them further when He tells them that it will be more bearable for Tyre and Sidon than for them on the day of judgment.

Tyre and Sidon were two Gentile cities where pagan worship and the worship of false gods were prominent. They were hedonistic cities and antagonistic toward Israel. Numerous prophets of the Old Testament such as Amos, Jeremiah, Joel, and Isaiah spoke of the wickedness in those cities. Tyre and Sidon were the types of places religious people would boycott, religious writers would write editorial pieces against, politicians would use as a way to point to the better way of life on our side of the world, and families would thank God they were not like "the people over there."

And yet Jesus tells the religious of Chorazin and Bethsaida that they will have a worse fate in the end. It is the equivalent of Jesus' walking into a church this Sunday and telling religious people who do not repent that judgment will be more bearable for the cross-dressing transvestite on Bourbon Street than it will be for the knowledgeable yet unrepentant church member sitting in the worship service. Jesus went on to drive home the point:

> "And you, Capernaum, will you be exalted to heaven?
> You will go down to Hades. For if the miracles that
> were done in you had been done in Sodom, it would
> have remained until today. But I tell you, it will be more
> tolerable for the land of Sodom on the day of judgment
> than for you." (Matt. 11:23–24)

Jesus contrasts Capernaum with Sodom but not in the way the people of Capernaum would imagine. Sodom no longer existed because God had destroyed it because of the vileness of its inhabitants. At one time God promised Abraham that if he could find just ten righteous people in the city, God would not destroy it. Instead, when God sent angels to check out the city, the men in the city surrounded the house where they were staying with the intentions of raping the angels. God rained burning sulfur on the city wiping out its existence.

To the people of Capernaum, Sodom was the epitome of evil. Yet Jesus steps into Capernaum and says that the wrath poured out on Sodom will be minuscule compared to the eternal wrath poured out on Capernaum.

Why did Jesus speak so strongly against the people of Capernaum? The people in this small town of Capernaum were exposed to Christ to a much greater degree than the people of Sodom. Therefore the people of Capernaum were more account- able because of their knowledge.

Capernaum was Jesus' home as an adult. In John 6:24, when people were searching for Jesus, they looked for Him in Capernaum. In Capernaum Jesus healed Peter's mother-in-law (Matt. 8:15), healed the sick who were brought to Him (Matt. 8:16), healed a paralyzed man who was lowered to Him on a mat (Mark 2:11), and taught in the synagogue and healed a man with an evil spirit amaz- ing all the people (Luke 4:35). Jesus preached the Sermon on the Mount right outside of Capernaum, and He delivered His famous "Living Bread" sermon in one of the synagogues in the city.

Matthew 9 reads like a highlight reel of just one day of Jesus' ministry in Capernaum. As Jesus walked through the streets of Capernaum to raise Jairus's daughter to life, a woman who was bleeding for twelve years touched Jesus and was healed immedi- ately. Later Jesus arrived at Jairus's house, raised the girl to life, and on His way out healed two blind men. He then healed a mute man possessed with a demon; and when the man spoke, the people said, "Nothing like this has ever been seen in Israel" (Matt. 9:33).

The people of Capernaum witnessed so much and repented so little (v. 20). Jesus was as offended with the self-righteous sin of Capernaum as He was with the overt wickedness of Sodom. For

Jesus, knowledge without repentance is just as wicked as blatant sinful living.

Jesus did not rebuke them for their knowledge. He rebuked them for their lack of repentance based on their knowledge. Knowledge of Christ will either condemn us or change us.

For the people in these cities, it would have been better if they had never been exposed to Jesus at such an extreme level. It would have been better for them not to hear His sermons in their synagogues, observe His miracles in their homes, and watch Him live among them. They were condemned by their own knowledge.

Jesus' sermon sounds crazy at first, doesn't it? Judgment will be harsher for the nice neighbor in Capernaum who lets his friends borrow his fishing gear than for the guy who wanted to rape the angels in Sodom. To put Jesus' teaching in our context, judgment will be harsher for the good guy who "endures" hundreds of sermons without truly following Jesus than for the terrorist who has limited knowledge of Christ.

How can this be?

The level of judgment is based on knowledge, not on wickedness. On the wickedness scale, we are all ruined before a fully righteous God because we all fall woefully short of His perfection. But on the knowledge scale, we have differing levels of exposure to Christ. Knowledge makes us accountable because it puts us in a position where we must respond. The more knowledge we have, the greater the accountability we owe. This truth should be terrifying to those of us reading in highly exposed cultures like the United States where there is an abundance of biblical information and a prominent Christian subculture.

> **Knowledge makes us accountable because it puts us in a position where we must respond.**

Leading a ministry that approaches discipleship as merely information and not repentance devalues discipleship and denies the power of the gospel. It is what Dietrich Bonhoeffer called "cheap grace."

> Cheap grace is the grace we bestow on ourselves.
> Cheap grace is the preaching of forgiveness without requiring repentance, baptism without church discipline, Communion without confession. . . . Cheap grace is grace without discipleship, grace without the cross, grace without Jesus Christ, living and incarnate.[5]

Deeper than Behavior Modification

Another faulty view of discipleship that plagues many churches is approaching discipleship as behavior modification. If you are a leader with this predisposition, you think the solution to a discipleship deficiency is teaching people to live "better." If you tend to focus on behavior, remember that Jesus has always focused on the heart.

In the Gospel of Mark, a young, well-respected man with exemplary behavior realizes he cannot be Jesus' disciple.

> As He was setting out on a journey, a man ran up, knelt down before Him, and asked Him, "Good Teacher, what must I do to inherit eternal life?" "Why do you call Me good?" Jesus asked him. "No one is good but One—God. You know the commandments: Do not murder; do not commit adultery; do not steal; do not bear false witness; do not defraud; honor your father and mother." He said to Him, "Teacher, I have kept all these from my youth." Then, looking at him, Jesus loved him and said to him,

"You lack one thing: Go, sell all you have and give to the poor, and you will have treasure in heaven. Then come, follow Me." But he was stunned at this demand, and he went away grieving, because he had many possessions. (Mark 10:17–22)

At first glance Jesus' response is surprising because the young man comes to Jesus in humility, falling on his knees before Him, yet Jesus allows him to leave without eternal life. He comes to the right person with the right question, but he leaves empty. Why?

He missed discipleship and eternal life because he was unwilling to give everything up to follow Jesus, but there is also another reason. He trusted in his own moral goodness. At some point in his life he was discipled on how to live without understanding his profound need for a Savior. His behavior was modified, but his heart was never changed. Perhaps he sat through "discipleship classes" that focused on how to be a better _____ but never challenged his heart.

Other Gospel writers indicate that the man was young, wealthy, and a ruler. His life appeared to be set; but despite all his influence and affluence, something was missing. And he knew it. All the stuff he had accumulated had not delivered on the promise of true life, so he wanted to know how to obtain eternal life. The Jews understood eternal life to include heaven but also inner peace, a sense of purpose, joy, and fulfillment. He ran to Jesus and essentially said, "Just tell me what to do!"

In His response Jesus makes a veiled claim to His deity. "Why do you call Me good? No one is good but One—God." In essence Jesus is saying, "You call me good. Only God is good. Either I am not good because I am not God. Or I am good and I am God. And because I am God, I am more than a teacher who can answer your question, but I am also the only One who can actually give you what you are looking for."

Jesus lists five of the Ten Commandments to lead the young man to a realization of his sin and need for a Savior. But with amazing self-deception the young man really believes he has kept all of the Commandments. He knows something is missing in his life, yet he feels he can remedy the problem by his own good deeds. He has excelled at everything in his life and believes that with just a little more guidance from Jesus he can behave his way into eternal life.

Jesus saw the young man's moralistic pride and still loved him. Jesus invited him to sell everything and follow Him. With such a specific command, Jesus was revealing the idol in the young man's heart and exposing the reality that he was not as good as he thought.

The young man claimed he obeyed the Commandments perfectly. But what he failed to realize is that all the rest of the Commandments flow from the first, "You shall have no other gods before me." Jesus showed the man that he has been in constant violation of the First Commandment. Money has been his god. His own morality has been his guide.

Instead of allowing the Commandments to lead him to his need for a Savior, he used them to prove his righteousness. The wealthy young ruler was flawed, as we all are, but he did not realize it. His problem was not his lack of goodness. His problem was he would not admit his lack of goodness.

Believing eternal life is something to be earned by his own merit, he approached Jesus and asked, "What must I *do* to inherit eternal life?" But the Christian faith is not something we do. It is something that was done for us by Christ. We receive eternal life not on our efforts but on His effort. We receive life not on our work but on His work on the cross.

Regretfully the young man goes away sad, realizing his goodness is imperfect and his heart is desperately attached to the god that will never quench him. He wanted to offer Jesus his behavior, but Jesus wanted his heart. He wanted another command to check off his daily list, but Jesus demanded his life.

Sadly, he would be a good member in many churches, faithfully looking for more things "to do" without his heart being challenged by the holiness and grace of God.

If a church views discipleship as merely tweaking behavior, then their work is contrary to the content of the gospel and the way of Jesus. Go after hearts. God does not desire to tweak our behavior. He desires to transform our lives.

Discipleship is transformation, not information overload or behavioral modification. When transformation occurs, there is an increasing hunger for more knowledge of Jesus and His Word, but the primary focus of acquiring knowledge must be the ongoing renewal of the heart. When transformation occurs, behavior will follow. But the focus must be the heart, or the behavior is self-manipulated and short-lived as opposed to flowing from the transformation offered by Christ.

Transformed Hearts

Jonathan Edwards preached during the first Great Awakening, the greatest revival in American history. God used him uniquely, and many people came to faith in Christ through his ministry. But several years later many believed that some who claimed to have become Christians during the Great Awakening were not true disciples. There was no change, no transformation. The lives of many of those supposedly converted appeared to be the same as before the Great Awakening. In response Edwards wrote his famous *Treatise on Religious Affections* to address the issue of deficient discipleship, of inauthentic faith. In his writing he coined the phrase "holy affections" as the distinguishing mark of true discipleship. He wrote: "The supreme proof of a true conversion is holy affections, zeal for holy things, longings after God, longings after holiness, desires for purity."

The distinguishing mark of Christian discipleship is a transformed heart, transformed affections. When someone becomes a true disciple, Christ radically changes the person's appetite.

When I (Eric) was in elementary school, I craved McDonalds. Often I begged my parents to have a McDonalds hamburger for dinner. If someone had told me that a day would come when I would have the freedom and resources to eat McDonalds every day of my life, I would have thought you were describing the new heaven and the new earth. McDonalds every day sounded like pure bliss.

But my affections changed.

In college I had two taste-bud-altering experiences. First, while visiting another country, I was overjoyed to discover a local McDonalds. However, after devouring lunch one day, including the lettuce washed in unpurified water, I became very sick. My stomach was in an upheaval for twenty-four consecutive hours. And with each hour I lost more and more of my appetite for McDonalds. When I returned home and drove past a McDonalds, all desire was gone for their burgers or fries. I was actually repulsed by what I formerly craved.

Second, someone took me to an expensive restaurant and introduced me to prime steak. Until that moment I was unaware that there are three distinct grades of steak: "select" is the lowest, followed by "choice," and then culminating in "prime." Less than 3 percent of all meat carries the distinguished and well-deserving title of "prime." When I first tasted a prime filet mignon cut of meat, I knew eating McDonalds would never be the same again.

It has been nearly fifteen years since I have eaten at McDonalds. I am not anti-McDonalds. My taste buds have just radically changed. I now have no desire for what I thought was the apex of culinary delights. What I once loved has lost its appeal. I love now what I once did not know. Granted, I could still eat McDonalds, but it will not satisfy as it once did because I have tasted much better.

The same has happened to believers on a much deeper, more spiritual level. Formerly we craved the created things rather than the Creator. We continually longed to taste that which was never meant to satisfy us. We ate the less glorious until our stomachs were full instead of feasting on the Glorious One. But because God is rich in mercy, Christ changed us and awakened us to the goodness that is in Him. We tasted the goodness of God, and our taste buds changed. We can still eat the things of this world. We just don't want to as we once did. He has transformed us; thus we prefer Him and His goodness because only He satisfies.

Don't settle for information or behavioral modification. Aim for Christ-centered discipleship that brings about true transformation.

2
Disciple to Win

He [a believer] still has plenty of business at the throne of grace: in fact, his business there increases rather than diminishes.
—Jonathan Edwards

A PAINFUL MOMENT HAPPENED during the 2011 NBA Finals. It was game two, and the Miami Heat was scorching the Dallas Mavericks. After winning the first game, the Heat jumped ahead by sixteen points with just over five minutes left in the game. It seemed certain they were going to take a commanding two to nothing lead over the Mavericks.

At this moment Eric sent a triumphant text to Josh Patterson, one of the lead pastors at the Village Church in Dallas. The text sent at 10:19 p.m. EST read:

Dallas is not doing bad for a JV team. It's nice for the league to let them play in the Finals. Usually JV has to play after the freshman game on Monday nights. I hope Dallas fans are understanding of the impossible likelihood of beating such a superior team.

What happened over the next several minutes is horrifying to recount for Heat fans and humiliating for the author of the above text message. The Mavs staged one of the greatest comebacks in NBA history to win game two and defeat the Heat in six games to win the NBA championship. Josh snapped a picture of the text and posted it on Twitter for thousands to see with the words, "Thanks Geiger, you made this too easy."

Up by sixteen points the Heat stopped playing to win and started playing to not lose. They started playing basketball's version of prevent defense. Fans hate prevent defense because teams historically blow big leads. And it's boring. With prevent defense the team assumes they will win. In their mind they don't need to score any more points; they just need to protect what they already have.

There is mammoth difference between *offensive discipleship* and *defensive discipleship*. And a leader's approach reveals his theology about the heart of people.[1]

Defensive discipleship plays to not lose the hearts of people to the world because defensive discipleship believes the hearts of people are pure. Consequently defensive discipleship focuses primarily on protecting people from influences in the world, from anything that could corrupt the perceived purity of the heart. Defensive discipleship strategy is prevalent and ranges from teaching people to isolate themselves from the culture to constantly alerting people of the influences they should avoid.

While defensive discipleship may sound appealing to some, it is theologically inaccurate. Our hearts are not pure in need of protection; they are wicked in need of transformation.

We are sinful from birth, sinful from the time we are conceived. We are born diseased and tainted with sin. We don't always prefer to be reminded or to remind others of

> *Our hearts are not pure in need of protection; they are wicked in need of transformation.*

this truth. No sane and loving person looks at a baby and says, "Aw—congratulations on your brand-new seven pound ball of sin. I brought you a stroller so you can roll that sin baby around." But it is true.

Defensive discipleship monitors behavior and plays defense. Sadly time reveals that the tweaked behavior was never grounded in a transformed heart. Offensive discipleship is different. It seeks primarily not to *protect* people from the world but to empower believers to *overcome* the world. Offensive discipleship understands the power of the gospel, trusts the regenerating power of the Holy Spirit, and knows that if Jesus brings His transformation, obedience will be the joyful result. Certainly offensive discipleship includes some protecting as the apostle Paul warned about wolves threatening to hurt sheep, but protection is not the end goal— heart change is the goal.

The Depth of Our Sin

Offensive discipleship is necessary because our hearts are more depraved than we can understand. King David loved God deeply, wrote incredible songs of praise to God, and was known as a man after God's own heart (Acts 13:22). Yet in Psalm 51, he gives us a glimpse into the depths of his soul. He confesses his desperate need for God's transforming work on his heart.

The back story to Psalm 51 begins in 2 Samuel 11.

> In the spring when kings march out to war, David sent Joab with his officers and all Israel. They destroyed the Ammonites and besieged Rabbah, but David remained in Jerusalem. (2 Sam. 11:1)

The first verse gives the reader a clue that something horrible is about to happen. Joab was David's top military adviser and someone who would have spoken truth in David's life. With Joab and all the military men gone, David is isolated. Not only is he isolated, but he is also in the wrong place. As the king of Israel, he was supposed to be at war. Instead he stayed behind.

> One evening David got up from his bed and strolled around on the roof of the palace. From the roof he saw a woman bathing—a very beautiful woman. So David sent someone to inquire about her, and he reported, "This is Bathsheba, the daughter of Eliam and wife of Uriah the Hittite." David sent messengers to get her, and when she came to him, he slept with her. . . . Afterward, she returned home. The woman conceived and sent word to inform David, "I am pregnant." (2 Sam. 11:2–5)

The rest of the story reads like the script of a movie. David sends for Uriah, Bathsheba's husband, to come meet with him. David engages in some small talk with Uriah, asking him about battle and the troops. But his real agenda is sending Uriah to his own house, where he hopes he will sleep with his own wife and the sin will be covered. David probably impresses himself with the ingenuity of the plan.

But Uriah sleeps outside of the palace because he thinks of his fellow soldiers sleeping on the battlefield. David hears that Uriah did not go home to bed so moves to plan B. He invites Uriah over again, but this time he gets him drunk. Surely the strong drink will cause Uriah to lose his inhibitions and self-control and go home to his wife, but Uriah once again sleeps outside the palace.

So David configures another plan, one much more diabolical in nature, but one he believes must be done to protect his reputation. David sends Uriah back to the battleground with a letter for Joab. Uriah did not realize that he carried his own death certificate, as Joab is ordered to place Uriah on the front lines of the battle and pull men back from the front lines so that Uriah will be left alone. The plan is initiated and Uriah dies on the battlefield. His death came by the enemy but was devised by David.

God sends the prophet Nathan to confront David. Nathan tells David a story about a rich man who owned tons of sheep and a poor man who had one lamb. The rich man had a guest one night; and instead of killing one of his many sheep, he reached over the fence and stole the one lamb from the poor man living next door. David is furious and wants to know who this man is. David, as king, is going to respond to such an injustice. He cannot fathom that someone's heart could be so cold. Like David, we tend to be much more frustrated with the sin we see in others than the sin in our own lives. Nathan says to David in 2 Samuel 12:7, "You are the man!"

The humbling confrontation with the holiness of God brings David to repentance. He records his prayer and plea for forgiveness in Psalm 51. The first few verses reveal the depth of his sin and our sin. Martin Luther wrote that in Psalm 51, like no other place in the Bible, we see the gravity of our sin.[2] We learn how devastating sin is, that there is no way to conquer it in our own goodness, and that our hearts can only be made new by Christ.

> Be gracious to me, God, according to Your faithful love; according to Your abundant compassion, blot out my rebellion (*pasha*). Wash away my guilt (*avah*) and cleanse me from my sin (*chatha*). (Ps. 51:1–2)

Did you notice what David does not address in his prayer? With the adulterous affair with Bathsheba as the prologue to this psalm, some would think sex would be mentioned in the psalm. There is not a word in the entire psalm about sex and not because the Bible is afraid to mention sex. David does not pray for his sexual purity, for God to protect his eyes, or for God to give him men to hold him accountable. He does not pray for sexual restraint because ultimately sex is not the issue. His heart is the issue.

The heart is the issue for each of us. It is the issue if we are the leader or the follower, the pastor or the member, the parent or the child. The heart is what matters to God.

By understanding Psalm 51, we can understand how sin corrupts our hearts. In the first two verses, David uses three different words to describe the comprehensive and devastating nature of sin.

In verse 1 David uses the Hebrew word *pasha*, which we translate "rebellion." Transgression is willful rebellion against one we owe allegiance to. David purposefully stayed home from war when his duty as king was to be with his men. David knowingly sent for Bathsheba when a servant cautioned him about her marital status. He knew in his heart he was rebelling against God, but he continued.

Rebellion occurs when a father asks his son to take out the trash on the all-important eve of trash day. The son ignores his father's instruction and goes to bed. Or he tells his father no as he walks out of the room. We severely discount the seriousness of sin if we describe sin as a mistake. Rebellion is much more than making a mistake, much deeper than forgetting to return a phone call or misplacing your car keys.

In verse 2 David uses the word *guilt* from the Hebrew word *avah*, which means "twisted out of shape." David is saying, "God, the problem with my heart is that it was not centered on You."

On the rooftop that dreaded night, David's heart is restless and twisted. He is not satisfied and quenched in God so he was looking for something else to satisfy him. Perhaps he longs for comfort because he feels alone. But instead of finding comfort in God, his heart is twisted, and he seeks comfort in the arms of Bathsheba. Perhaps he is overwhelmed with the responsibility of being king, but instead of trusting God with his burdens, his heart is twisted and he seeks an escape. Perhaps his heart is twisted and he feels the need to conquer something or control something, and he sees Bathsheba as an opportunity to wield his power.

This is the same David who prayed while hiding in a cave from Saul, "Be gracious to me, God, be gracious to me, for I take refuge in You" (Ps. 57:1). But not now. On the roof his heart twisted out of shape and is running to something else, to someone else.

Avah is a deeply convicting and challenging word because it speaks to the motivation of our hearts. It means we can do the right things for the wrong reasons. A father asks his son to take out the trash on the eve of trash day. The son jumps off the couch and empties every single trash can, even refilling them with plastic bags. But on this night the son takes out the trash for himself not for his father; he hopes his father will let him stay up late to watch more TV. He does the right action but for the wrong reason. Someone may appear to do the right things while his heart is filled with iniquity.

You may look at us and think we are pure-hearted pastors. Maybe that is true. But maybe we enjoy being a pastor because we need to be needed and our hearts are twisted out of shape as we find our worth in our roles and not in Christ. You may observe one of us with our children and say, "Look at him loving and leading his family well." Maybe that is true. Or maybe the heart is twisted and has replaced God with a child for the source of ultimate joy. You may see one of us exercise (this one is far less likely) and think, "He is managing his health well." Maybe that is true. Or maybe our values have twisted out of shape and caloric intake and exercise regimen are the last thoughts before bed and the first thoughts in the morning.

When you dive into the word *avah*, you realize the depth of your sin is deeper than you first imagined. The famous philosopher Søren Kierkegaard captured the concept of iniquity when he wrote, "Sin is finding identity in anything other than God."[3]

The third word David uses in verse 2 to show the all-encompassing nature of sin is the word *chatha*, which we translate *sin*. *Chatha* paints the picture of missing the mark or missing the target. Think of the illustration again about a father asking his son to take out the trash. The son rushes through the job, does not empty the bathroom trash cans, drags the kitchen trash on the floor making a complete mess, and does not bother putting a new trash bag in the kitchen trash can. A task has been accomplished, but the boy's attempt misses the mark of his father's reasonable standard.

When David lusted after Bathsheba, he missed the mark of God's holy love. When he plotted Uriah's murder, he fell woefully short of God's sovereignty and providence. When he attempted the elaborate cover-up, he violated the standard of God's truthfulness.

Broken Disciples

We learn from David's self-disclosure that our hearts, and the hearts of the people we serve, are in desperate need of transformation. We need offensive discipleship.

"But wait," one may argue, "Psalm 51 is not for me. My sin is not like David's."

If someone feels he doesn't need the prayer of Psalm 51, he doesn't fully understand the depth of his sin. Our sin is constantly before us (v. 3) as we were sinful from birth (v. 5). We continually need the restoration and cleansing David finds. Transformed disciples continually repent, continually pray prayers similar to Psalm 51.

But shouldn't we pray Psalm 51 less and less the more we are transformed?

Absolutely not. Rather than less and less, we will be in the middle of it more and more. We don't need grace less the longer we are His but more. The closer we get to Him, we realize the depth of His holiness is more than we previously understood. Consequently our sinfulness is more sinful than we ever

> **We don't need grace less the longer we are His but more.**

imagined. We will understand that His grace must be greater than we ever knew. Without a greater understanding of His grace, the increased realization of our sin crushes us.

Not only can we learn from David's self-examination of his heart, but we should also learn from his response to his sin. David's is the response of a true disciple who knows God and is continually being transformed by Him, even in facing his sin. To bring people to a point of transformation, leaders must lead people to repent as David repents. When confronted with the holiness of God and our sinfulness, how do we respond? How do we lead people to respond?

David does not respond with blame.

He says to God, "Against You—You alone—I have sinned" (v. 4). He does not shift blame to anyone. Noticeably absent in the text are common excuses:

My men should have stopped me.

I cannot help myself.

She was bathing on the stinking roof. Who does that?

My wife Michal was not what I needed her to be; she drove my heart elsewhere.

David offers none of these stupid excuses. He accepts full responsibility. Offensive discipleship includes insisting people accept full responsibility for their sin by, as an act of grace, refusing to accept foolish excuses.

David does not attempt to bargain with God.

David does not say, "Let me make it up to You, God. Let me give You some sacrifices." Conversely, he prays, "You do not want a sacrifice, or I would give it" (v. 16).

People often attempt to bargain with God. "I don't invest in my children so I will make it up with gifts. I don't give so I will volunteer more. I don't live pure during the week so I will sing real loud at church, God." Offensive discipleship continually reminds people that God wants our hearts, not our bargain offerings.

I (Philip) often teach that the difference here is between viewing our relationship with God as full surrender rather than a treaty. In a treaty nations keep their individual sovereignty and trade favors with one another. Not so in our walk with Christ. He calls for our total surrender, and no bargaining is allowed. He is King and we are not. We have no leverage point to decide what ought to happen next in life, what is declared righteous, or what is allowable in our lives.

David also does not believe in himself.

David knows the solution is not forgiving himself; he needs God's forgiveness. He knows he cannot fix the problem of his heart, so he prays, "God, create a clean heart for me" (v. 10), and, "Restore the joy of Your salvation to me" (v. 12)—not my salvation but Yours because I am incapable of rescuing or changing my heart.

Sadly defensive discipleship enables people to respond with blame (my sins are a result of my surrounding influences), bargain (I will make it up to God) or belief in self (I can do better next time). Defensive discipleship is a vicious cycle of deception and defeat based on a faulty theology.

David responds with brokenness.

Like all disciples in the process of transformation, he prays, "Let me hear joy and gladness; let the bones You have crushed rejoice" (v. 8). When we encounter His love and holiness, we are joyfully broken—realizing that His grace is all we need. Transformation occurs when we live in brokenness, constantly in awe of His grace and holiness. David realizes that "the sacrifice pleasing to God is a broken spirit. God, You will not despise a broken and humbled heart" (v. 17).

David responds to the holiness of God and the realization of his sinfulness with brokenness. He hates his sin but not himself. He knows he is deeply loved by God, giving him the confidence to pray the bold prayer of Psalm 51. At the same time he is fully broken over the sin in his life. Offensive discipleship challenges people to live as broken disciples before Him by applying the holiness and grace of God to the heart.

Obviously we are building the case that transformational discipleship is about the heart, much more significant than merely mastering biblical information or behavioral modification. And we believe that those who make transformed disciples play offense not defense, constantly applying the grace of God to people's hearts for true transformation.

Obedience Is Better

God assured David that His transforming work on David's heart would result in obedience. David commits to "teach the rebellious [God's] ways" (v. 13) and "declare [God's] praise" (v. 15). He develops a passion for his city to be reconciled to God (vv. 18–19). David was keenly aware that God desires obedience flowing from a transformed heart. He served as king during Israel's sacrificial system and knew God ultimately delights in obedience (vv. 16–17).

Talk is often cheap. Real faith and real transformation are accompanied by real action. Though transformation occurs in the heart, it is validated by obedience. Jesus couldn't have been much more explicit about this fact: "If you love Me, you will keep My commands" (John 14:15).

> *Real faith and real transformation are accompanied by real action.*

The temptation for leaders is to hide behind the heart and refuse to confront sinful behavior. We pass off the responsibility to directly address wrongdoing with the spiritual sounding claim that we are not to judge because, after all, God alone knows the heart.

True enough. But though we cannot know another's heart, we can hold tightly to the truth that a transformed heart results in a transformed life (1 John 2:3; 5:3). Someone who is being transformed by God displays fruits of the Spirit (Gal. 5:22–23) as spiritual fruit is a byproduct of a heart that repents (Matt. 3:8). Those without fruit reveal that their hearts have not yet been transformed (Matt. 7:18).

So while being primarily concerned with the hearts of the people under your care, realize that a lack of spiritual fruit fundamentally reveals the need for transformation.

Don't Shrug at the Grass

Multiple summers I (Eric) have come home from vacation to massive spots in my lawn that are completely parched. I am not referring to small spots that can be corrected with a few patches of grass; I mean embarrassingly ruined sections of my lawn that cause my neighbors to cast looks of sympathy my way because my house has potentially lost value (as if it needed help). Dissatisfaction with my lawn in those moments is high. The grass is not fruitful, not vibrant as it should be. The neighbors don't see a yard as it should be seen.

Imagine the people in your church as a lawn, a field. The apostle Paul gave this image in 1 Corinthians 3:9 telling the Corinthian Christians they were "God's field, God's building." How does the yard look?

If there are dry and parched sections in your church, hopefully your heart is filled with much greater dissatisfaction for the level of deficient disciples than for a subpar lawn. Perhaps you are thinking of some of the people who sit in your church, those whose lives seem parched. Maybe you are frustrated with the lack of passion in worship, apathy toward the Scripture, an inward focus, the grip of materialism, childish men, or failing marriages.

The pain of continually staring at parched lives is deep—that is, if you care.

Some don't care. Some leaders are consumed with creating a bigger field, even if it's a parched field. Other leaders mask the lack of life with the multitude of activities on the church schedule. Size and activity often cover immaturity. Some leaders have given up the dream of leading a movement of people transformed by Christ. They have become apathetic chaplains of a mediocre institution.

> *The pain of continually staring at parched lives is deep—that is, if you care.*

If you don't care, repent. If you do care, be careful.

If your heart is filled with anguish for the massive parched patches in the field God has entrusted to you, be careful not to paint the lawn. Be careful that your God-given desire for a church filled with people whose lives are bearing fruit is not quenched with a cheap and temporary substitution.

Don't Paint the Lawn

One summer evening, after staring at dead patches in my yard, I searched online for a solution and discovered many products that would "paint my lawn green." The lawn paint does not cause new growth, restore life to the roots, or foster a healthy yard. It merely masks the sickness. It is a facade to give the impression of life when there is nothing but death. While some may be tempted to order the paint, it is a temporary solution to a deeper problem.

My lawn did not need paint. My lawn needed life. My lawn needed nurture in the forms of water and fertilizer. It would be ludicrous to remedy the external look of my lawn and declare it healthy.

In the same way it is ludicrous for a church to teach for behavior rather than teach for the heart. We must be careful that our desire for spiritual fruit does not lead us to seek to teach for fruitfulness apart from transformation. But it happens all the time. Here is one example . . .

A church leader attends a worship gathering at a conference and perceives the people are more passionate than the people in his church. So he takes mental notes of the hungry expressiveness and the postures of reverence. He comes back to his church with a conclusion that worship "looks this way" so he teaches people to act a certain way in a worship gathering. Instead of reminding people of the greatness of God and His goodness expressed to them in Jesus, he paints a picture of what worship should "look like." Instead of trusting that as God refreshes hearts with what Christ has *done* authentic worship will flow, he gives specifics on what people should *do* in the worship gathering. Instead of teaching for heart transformation, he teaches for behavior. It is easier to measure, and the immediate result is tempting.

Months later many in the congregation have learned how to physically emulate the response the leader is teaching. Yet the leader painfully wonders if hearts have truly been transformed. The grass looks greener, but it is not truly green.

Don't shrug at the brown grass, but don't paint it either.

The symptoms of unhealthy lawn should alert us that there is a problem, but it would be foolish to treat only the symptoms. The parched lawn is a concern, but the root issue of unhealthiness must be addressed rather than an external issue such as texture or color. As a church leader, you must be concerned with the dry spots in the field. But you must not paint the dry spots green. Or teach the dry spots to act green.

Be deeply concerned when you see evidence of deficient discipleship. Allow the lack of fruit and the parched lives to break your heart. Allow God to fill you with His burden and passion for the people He loves. Don't shrug off the responsibility, but don't disciple for behavior either.

> *Play aggressive offense, not passive defense.*

Play aggressive offense, not passive defense. Disciple for transformed hearts, knowing that transformation always results in obedience.

3
Transformational Sweet Spot

What each one honors before all else, what before all things he admires and loves, this for him is God.

—Origen

THUS FAR WE HAVE established that everyone is a disciple of someone, but only disciples of Jesus are transformed. We have understood Christian discipleship to be ultimately about transformation rather than merely information or behavior modification, and the best way to see transformation is through offensive discipleship—to apply the grace of Jesus to people's hearts.

So how do we play offense?

How do we train people to *overcome* the world and not drift toward a discipleship model that merely seeks to *protect* people from the world? Scottish pastor Thomas Chalmers wrote:

The best way to overcome the world is not with morality or self-discipline. Christians overcome the world by seeing the beauty and excellence of Christ. They overcome the world by seeing something more attractive than the world: Christ.[1]

Someone who has tasted the wonder of Ruth's Chris steak-house does not crave Golden Corral. Someone who has spent the night in a Ritz does not crave the bed in a Motel Six. Someone who has enjoyed a summer vacation in Hawaii does not crave a week at the local swimming pool. When someone truly encounters the beauty of Jesus, the things of this world are not nearly as attractive. Transformational discipleship occurs when people are impressed with the attractiveness of Christ and confronted with the deficiency of lesser gods.

Please don't misread. We don't make Christ attractive; we don't make Him awesome. We don't make Him better than the world. He already is. We simply help others see the greatness of God.

God Versus Gods

To remind God's people of the greatness of God, the psalmist compares God with the gods/idols of his day.

> Not to us, Yahweh, not to us, but to Your name give glory
> because of Your faithful love, because of Your truth. Why
> should the nations say, "Where is their God?" Our God
> is in heaven and does whatever He pleases. Their idols
> are silver and gold, made by human hands. They have
> mouths but cannot speak, eyes, but cannot see. They have
> ears but cannot hear, noses, but cannot smell. They have
> hands but cannot feel, feet, but cannot walk. They cannot
> make a sound with their throats. Those who make them
> are just like them, as are all who trust in them. Israel,

trust in the LORD! He is their help and shield. House of
Aaron, trust in the LORD! He is their help and shield. You
who fear the LORD, trust in the LORD! He is their help
and shield. (Ps. 115:1–11)

In the psalmist's context the idols were lifeless miniature statues, but idolatry occurs when anything created grabs the attention
of a person's heart more than the Creator. Idolatry is often taking
something good in our life and making it our God. For example,
marriage, parenthood, career, and leisure are good gifts from God
but terrible gods. They cannot satisfy as God satisfies because they
are not God, and they cannot withstand the pressure of being God.
Thus when we make a good thing our God, we saddle that good
thing with unrealistic expectations and everyone loses.

The psalmist knew, as John Calvin wrote, "That man's nature,
so to speak, is a perpetual factory of idols. After the Flood there
was a sort of rebirth of the world, but not many years passed by
before men were fashioning gods according to their pleasure."[2]
Because of our tendency to become impressed with gods more
than God, the psalmist compares the attractiveness and power of
God to the deficiency and impotence of the gods.

The psalmist establishes that God is the timeless Creator who
is in heaven and does whatever He pleases while the gods are tem-
poral creations, made with human hands. The word the psalmist
uses for God is *Yahweh*, which means "the self-existing one." He is,
has always been, and will always be. The idols in the psalmist's day
are already gone; gods come and go as quickly as tight-rolled jeans
and, prayerfully, skinny jeans, too.

The imagery in the text is incredible. The idols have mouths
that cannot speak, but God spoke the world into existence (Ps.
33:9) and speaks still to His children. Idols, the statues in the

psalmist's day, have carved eyes that cannot see, but God sees and brings strength to His own (2 Chron. 16:9). Idols have ears that cannot hear; they are unable to respond with power. The prophets of Baal painfully learned that the gods cannot hear, but the God of Elijah hears and responds (1 Kings 18).

The text says the gods have noses but cannot smell. In the ancient Jewish sacrificial system, the phrase had additional meaning because the Scriptures taught that God smelled the aroma of the sacrifices and was pleased with them (Num. 15:3). Worshipping a god who could not smell would be terrifying for the worshipper. If the god could not smell the sacrifice of the worshipper, consequently the sacrifice would never be enough because the god would never be satisfied. The god would always want and need more from the worshipper.

Still the gods are never satisfied, and they never satisfy.

If a career is god, the career will never be quenched, as it demands more time, energy, and sacrifice. If money is god, the bank account will never be fat enough. It will always want more and will never satisfy. If pornography is god, it will demand more focus and passion while never delivering on true satisfaction.

> **Still the gods are never satisfied, and they never satisfy.**

God smells and is satisfied. The Old Testament sacrificial system foreshadowed the ultimate sacrifice of Christ, which makes us pure before Him. God smells and is satisfied with us because of the sacrifice of Jesus. The gods say, "Give me more and more. Your sacrifices will never be finished." Jesus cried, "It is finished" as the righteous requirements of our holy God were perfectly fulfilled in the death of His Son.

The gods are completely powerless, with feet that cannot walk and a throat that cannot make a sound. God does whatever He pleases. As King Nebuchadnezzar discovered, "No god can save like our God" (Dan. 3).

To conclude the comparisons, the psalmist makes an epic statement in verse 8: *"Those who make [idols] are just like them, as are all who trust in them."* Idols are worthless and lifeless, and those who worship idols become worthless and lifeless (Jer. 2:5).

Everyone is a disciple and everyone is a worshipper; these are not exclusively Christian terms. Fyodor Dostoyevsky wrote in *The Brothers Karamazov,* "So long as man remains free he strives for nothing so incessantly and so painfully as to find someone to worship."[3] People have always looked for someone or something to follow, and people have always become like whoever or whatever they choose as their object of affection.

> **Everyone is a disciple and everyone is a worshipper.**

We become like the God/god we behold.

We appear like the God/god we admire.

We duplicate the God/god we deify.

We favor the God/god we follow.

We match the God/god we magnify.

Ruin or Restoration

We resemble the God/god we revere, and this will either be for our ruin or our restoration.[4] If the people we serve are not deeply impressed with Christ, the gods they serve will leave them ruined. They will live lifeless, worthless lives lacking the transformation only God can bring.

Augustine recounted a chilling story about a friend whose life was almost ruined by an idol in his culture. Alypius arrived in

Rome before Augustine did, and a prominent god in that culture was the savage gladiatorial events held at the coliseum where people hedonistically feasted on watching others die. At first Alypius refused the invitation from friends to attend the events, but he finally agreed to attend but with his eyes closed committing to "be there in body but absent in spirit." But Alypius heard the roar of the crowd when a fighter was killed, and Augustine wrote:

> He opened his eyes and was struck with a deeper wound
> in his soul than the victim whom he desired to see had
> been in his body. Thus he fell more miserably than the
> one whose fall had raised that mighty clamor which had
> entered through his ears and unlocked his eyes to make
> way for the wounding and beating down of his soul. . . . He
> was now no longer the same man who came in, but was
> one of the mob he came into, a true companion of those
> who had brought him thither. He looked, he shouted, he
> was excited, and he took away with him the madness that
> would stimulate him to come again: not only with those
> who first enticed him, but even without them; indeed,
> dragging in others besides.[5]

Alyipus began to resemble the calloused games that fascinated his heart. Idols always ruin us, always ruin the people under our spiritual care. This is why we must constantly point people to the attractiveness of Christ so that they realize He is so much greater than the gods of this world. In Psalm 16 David compares the sorrows the gods offer with the ultimate pleasure God offers.

> The sorrows of those who take another god for themselves
> will multiply; I will not pour out their drink offerings
> of blood, and I will not speak their names with my lips.

> LORD, You are my portion and my cup of blessing; You
> hold my future. . . . In Your presence is abundant joy; in
> Your right hand are eternal pleasures. (Ps. 16:4–5, 11)

Sadly we know verse 4 to be true. Sorrows always increase when we pursue another god. The temptation, the offer from a god for joy, and a brief season of pleasure follow, but in the end only misery remains. If we lust after another woman, our mind enjoys it for a moment, but sorrow increases as we are left empty. If we enter into a conversation that is full of gossip, we feel the rush of being trusted with insider information, but misery comes quickly as integrity is exchanged for a conversation. If our heart chases after material things, we enjoy them for a season, but the sorrows increase as the shine on the new toys wanes.

Augustine self-disclosed the sorrow he experienced while pursuing other gods. One night, before he became a follower of Christ, he was out with some friends, and a drunken beggar came to them for money. In their self-righteousness Augustine and his friends discussed the sad state of the beggar, but later Augustine realized he was just as miserable. He was attempting to find fulfillment in fame and knowledge, but he went to sleep each night unfulfilled. They both were searching for fleeting joy, the beggar in a bottle and himself in fame. Only the beggar actually had it better. At least he was numb to the pain. Augustine came to faith in Christ and wrote of the experience:

> I was still eagerly aspiring to honors, money, and
> matrimony; and You did mock me. In pursuit of these
> ambitions I endured the most bitter hardships, in which
> You were being the more gracious the less You would
> allow anything that was not You to grow sweet to me.[6]

God is good and gracious not to allow a lesser unsatisfying god even to come close to quenching us because abundant joy is in Him. C. S. Lewis said, "God cannot give us happiness and peace apart from Himself, because it is not there. There is no such thing."[7] David calls God his "cup" (Ps. 16:5) because he knows God is all he needs. David's heart is fascinated with the beauty and greatness of God—and this is transformational.

Sin happens for us and for the people we serve when we forget that God is enough, when we want something other than Him. Sin is telling God that we need something more than Him, that the god can bring greater joy than Him. Gossip is telling God that He is not enough, that we need the juicy information. Clicking on the porn site is telling God that He is not the cup, that the porn site is needed to bring excitement or escape. Chasing a promotion motivated by greed is telling God that He is not enough.

Only God is enough. Only God delivers on joy.

After reminding the people of the greatness of God and the impotence of the false gods, the psalmist implores the people to "trust in the LORD" (Ps. 115:9). He knows their transformation is related to their trust in God and their fascination with Him. We resemble the God or god we revere, and with Christ this is for our restoration. If the people you lead will treasure Christ, He will transform them. And they will be filled with ultimate and abundant joy. The famous mathematician Blaise Pascal wrote:

> All men seek happiness. This is without exception.
> Whatever different means they employ, they all tend to
> this end. The cause of some going to war, and of others
> avoiding it, is the same desire in both, attended with
> different views. . . . And yet after such a great number
> of years, no one without faith has reached the point to

which all continually look . . . because the infinite abyss can only be filled by an infinite and immutable Object, that is to say, only by God Himself."[8]

Theology of Transformation

As church leaders, we long to see transformation in the lives of people, our church, and our city. Alton Garrison of the Assemblies of God said when we were interviewing him, "Our mission is not complete until we have seen people have life change." The word from the Scriptures often associated with transformation is "metamorphosis." It communicates lasting and irreversible change at the core, not merely external alterations or tweaking the appearance. Metamorphosis is used to describe the process a caterpillar goes through to become a butterfly. The apostle Paul paints a picture of transformation:

> *Our mission is not complete until we have seen people have life change.*

> Now the Lord is the Spirit, and where the Spirit of the Lord is, there is freedom. We all, with unveiled faces, are looking as in a mirror at the glory of the Lord and are being transformed into the same image from glory to glory; this is from the Lord who is the Spirit. (2 Cor. 3:17–18)

Paul is taking the readers back to Moses and his encounters with God on Mount Sinai. Each time Moses met with God, he walked down the mountain transformed, glowing after enjoying the presence of God. Moses wore a veil over his face to cover the fact that the glory was fading (2 Cor. 3:13) because with each step away from the mountain, he stepped farther away from the presence of God.

Paul says that we believers have unveiled faces. The glory does not decrease for us as it did for Moses. Because we never leave the presence of God, the glory increases. We never leave the mountain because the Spirit is in us. We enjoy a relationship with God that even Moses did not have.

The language Paul uses is intentional—God is the one who does the transforming. We don't transform ourselves. We "are being transformed." All this, all the transforming, is "from the Lord who is the Spirit."

God desires to bring His people through this metamorphosis process. He seeks to transform the people in your church into His image, and He wants to do so with ever increasing glory. Meaning He wants the people you serve to be more like Him tomorrow than they are today.

If God does all the transforming, what is our part? If God is the one responsible to mature the people under your care, what is your role?

God transformed Moses, but Moses played a significant role in the transformation. His role was simple but still necessary.

He walked up the mountain.

Moses put himself in the right position to be transformed. He discovered the posture where God would move in his life, and he put himself there.

Some leaders and Christians drift toward *passivity* in their approach to spiritual transformation. They rightly believe that God is the one who transforms, but they wrongly assume zero responsibility for their maturation. The apostle Paul trusted God to do the transforming while simultaneously rejecting a passive approach to discipleship. He challenged Timothy to "train yourself in godliness" (1 Tim. 4:7) and strained toward the goal of Christlikeness (Phil. 3:13).

Other leaders and Christians drift to *performance* in their view of discipleship, as if we are the ones who transform ourselves. These leaders trade in their freedom in Christ for an updated version of the law filled with human regulations and legislated self-righteousness.

The proper perspective is neither passivity nor performance but *partnership*. Spiritual transformation is divine-human synergy over a lifetime.[9] As leaders we must teach that our reliance upon God does not preclude personal responsibility for obedience. God graciously commands His people humbly to put themselves in the right posture to be transformed, and He does the transforming. The divine-human synergy is well seen in Paul's encouragement to believers in Philippi:

> So then, my dear friends, just as you have always obeyed, not only in my presence, but now even more in my absence, work out your own salvation with fear and trembling. For it is God who is working in you, enabling you both to desire and to work out His good purpose. (Phil. 2:12–13)

If you have ever waterskied or kneeboarded, you understand partnership. You are not the one who lifts you out of the water or pulls you across the lake. The boat has all of the power. But you do play a part. You must place yourself in the right posture behind the boat, give the one driving the boat a thumbs-up sign, and prepare for the ride.

Spiritual transformation is the same. God is the one enabling His people to mature and grow while His people are invited to place themselves in the right posture.

Church ministry, like personal spiritual growth, is a divine-human partnership. As a church leader your role is not to transform people. You cannot, and it is offensive to God if you believe you can. Your role is to place people in the pathway of God's transforming power. Your leadership, preaching, teaching, investing, and counseling are to be instruments God uses for His holy endeavors to transform people. Those sacred practices must be used to show people how attractive Christ is so that people are positioned for transformation.

> *Your role is to place people in the pathway of God's transforming power.*

Eric and Philip were both involved in the research and the project for the book *Transformational Church*, where we learned from churches that are seeing significant transformation in the lives of the people they disciple. In our research we found that many church leaders in these "transformational churches" struggled with questions about discipleship programs or discipleship tools. They did not view discipleship as one "thing" they offer, whether a program or a strategy. Rather, making disciples is seen as the overarching reason they exist. They viewed disciple-making as their paramount calling with every activity being used as a pathway for transformation. To see God bring about metamorphosis in increasing numbers of people, these churches helped people live in what we now call the Transformational Sweet Spot.

The Sweet Spot

The Transformational Sweet Spot (TSS) is the centerpiece of the framework that was developed through a massive research project on discipleship. This book is the culmination of the intensive research project seeking to understand what kind of discipleship is truly transformational. The LifeWay Research team discovered that certain factors are at work in the lives of believers who are progressing in spiritual maturity. We refer to them as the attributes of discipleship.

1. Bible Engagement
2. Obeying God and Denying Self
3. Serving God and Others
4. Sharing Christ
5. Exercising Faith
6. Seeking God
7. Building relationships
8. Unashamed

The eight attributes are biblical factors that consistently show up in the life of a maturing believer. Throughout the proceeding chapters, we will highlight different attributes as they apply to believers moving into the TSS.

After carefully studying Scripture through the lens of discipleship, evaluating the research, interviewing godly leaders who have devoted their lives to seeing others discipled—we humbly offer the framework.

Please do not view this as a model.

Let us say that again: *please do not view this as a model.*

If you happen to be at an event where we speak about "transformational discipleship" and you ask us to unpack the "model," you will quickly learn that our personal transformation is far from complete as our frustration will be visible.

This is not a model.

I know we are being overly and painfully clear on this point, but Eric coauthored *Simple Church*, which was meant to challenge leaders to have a process for discipleship. It was never intended to be a model (the first paragraph of the book read, "This is not a model"), yet for the last five years many church leaders treated the book as a "new model" for church ministry. The church's proclivity for models alarmingly reveals our shallowness.

The same temptation for model-worship has been true of *Transformational Church*. Ed Stetzer and Thom Rainer did not want to offer a scheme that would simply sell more books, events, consulting, and all the rest. Instead, they wanted what we all want: to give church leaders an understanding of what will help more people become faithful disciples of Christ. To that end, both *Transformational Church* with its TC Loop and *Transformational Discipleship* with the TSS are driven not by a prescriptive model. Rather, we believe that transformation across all church models can occur by tapping into the right principles.

> *We believe that transformation across all church models can occur by tapping into the right principles.*

The transformational framework should not become your new mission statement, be placed in your bulletin, or hung on the wall in your auditorium. It should, however, impact your thinking on discipleship—your understanding of how people mature in your church. We humbly believe it should greatly impact your teaching, programming, leadership development, and availability to people during specific seasons in their lives. But you will need to listen to the voice of the Spirit as to the specific changes He is leading you to make in your ministry. Practice divine-human synergy as you interact with the transformational framework and Transformational Sweet Spot.

Transformational Framework

The Transformational Sweet Spot is the
intersection of truth given by healthy leaders when
someone is in a vulnerable posture.

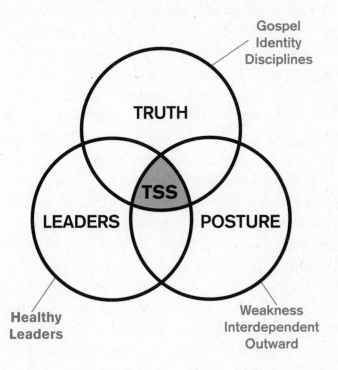

In sports, tennis rackets and baseball bats are known to have
"sweet spots." If the sweet spot connects with the ball, a powerful
hit is most likely to occur. In the audio industry the sweet spot
is the focal point between two speakers where the listener hears
music the way it was intended to be heard.

The Transformational Sweet Spot is the synergy of truth, posture, and leaders that helps a disciple see Christ as the only God

worthy of worship. The TSS occurs when *healthy leaders give truth to a disciple who is in a vulnerable posture.* We don't write this as a magic formula or a simplistic depiction of spiritual growth, as we know and believe God is the one who brings transformation. Transformation is the mysterious work of the Spirit. At the same time we are confident that He longs to transform His people, and we view the TSS as a humble attempt to articulate the position people are in as God brings His transforming work. As Billie Hanks has said, "I've never met a mature Christian, only maturing Christians." Let's help people move into that journey.

We heard many stories validating God's transforming work through the means of truth, leaders, and posture. Carol lost her husband in a tragic car accident. Prior to the accident she attended church and occasionally read her Bible but out of honesty would not have described herself as completely devoted to Christ. After the accident a strong Christian coworker came alongside Carol with comfort and encouragement. Over lunches and coffee breaks Carol's friend applied the truth of God to Carol's heart. She saw the greatness of God and the beauty of Christ, and her heart melted. A godly leader applied truth to her heart during a vulnerable season, and her faith began to soar.

James attended church for years. He thought he was committed to Christ. But his faith journey escalated quickly through an experience with his small group. For over a year he attended the small group and minimally engaged, remaining somewhat distant and protected. However, his small group decided to take a foreign mission trip together, and James's world flipped upside down. During the day he was humbled by what he saw and touched by the faith of the Christians in an impoverished country. At night he began to open up to other men in his small group. One of them James really respected.

Over a series of conversations, James's friend confronted James with the truth and challenged him to take his faith more seriously. James saw Christ as more desirable than the things of the world he had been chasing. His heart was crushed with the transforming grace of Christ, and he has not been the same since. His vulnerability with other men on a mission trip combined with receiving truth from a healthy leader put James in a position for deep transformation. To continue growing, James knows he must remain connected in true Christian community while constantly interacting with the truth of Jesus.

Think about your intense seasons of spiritual growth. Were you in a vulnerable posture? Did your heart encounter the truth of God? Was someone there alongside you to apply truth to your heart or walk with you through the challenging season?

Think of the seasons when you became stagnant in your faith. Did you lose your vulnerability and dependence on God? Were you no longer allowing the truth of God to challenge your heart?

In coming chapters we will unpack truth, leaders, and posture so you may evaluate how they interplay in your ministry context to help people see the attractiveness of Christ. We become like the God/god we behold. The people you serve are either being joyfully transformed by Him, or they are miserably transforming into the gods they treasure.

Part 1

Transformational Framework: TRUTH

The Transformational Sweet Spot is the intersection of truth given by healthy leaders to someone in a vulnerable posture.

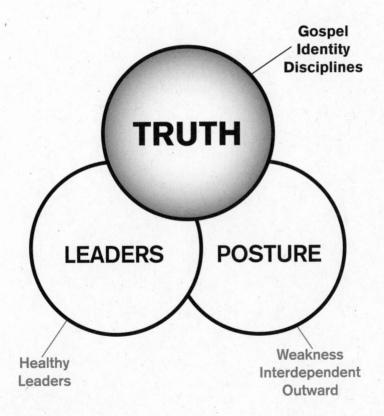

If you continue in My word, you really
are My disciples. You will know the truth,
and the truth will set you free.

(John 8:31–32)

• • •

Sanctify them by the truth, Your word is truth.

(John 17:17)

• • •

The Elder: To the elect lady [a local church]
and her children: I love all of you in the truth—and
not only I, but also all who have come to know the
truth—because of the truth that remains in us
and will be with us forever.

(2 John 1:1–2)

• • •

The one who says, "I have come to know Him,"
yet doesn't keep His commands, is a liar,
and the truth is not in him.

(1 John 2:4)

• • •

By His own choice, He gave us a new birth
by the message of truth so that we would be the
firstfruits of His creatures.

(James 1:18)

TRUTH

*Truth is incontrovertible, malice may attack it and
ignorance may deride it, but, in the end, there it is.*
—Sir Winston Churchill[10]

THE TRUTH OF GOD is undefiled and unchangeable, and God
has chosen to use His truth to bring transformation to His people.
By His truth we were saved and by His truth we are made holy
and walk in freedom. Quite simply, transformation does not occur
apart from the truth of God.

In relation to transformation, there are three important lenses
from which leaders see truth, three important lenses that contribute to transformation. The truth does not change as we look at it
through different lenses or from different angles, rather we see a
clearer understanding of God's truth.

The Gospel writers wrote four different accounts about the
same life of the living Truth—Jesus. These four Gospels do not
contradict one another in the slightest; rather they enhance our
understanding of Jesus.

The most foundational lens is the gospel. We will discover that
the gospel is for believers, that the gospel is sufficient not only for
justification but also for sanctification. People are transformed as
they encounter the gospel again and again. Leaders must view discipleship through the lens of the gospel and help their people constantly preach the gospel to themselves.

The second lens is the discipline lens; discipleship must also
be viewed through the lens of discipline. The Scripture challenges
believers to pursue God, to train themselves for godliness. Coupled

with an accurate understanding of the gospel and the new identity, spiritual disciplines are essential for transformation.

The third lens is the new identity of believers. As people realize the ramifications of the gospel in their lives—the reality that they have a new identity—they are empowered by the truth of their new character to live worthy of their new calling. Leaders must help people embrace the truth of their new identity.

In the movie *National Treasure*, the heroes and the villains are searching for a treasure hidden somewhere in the United States. All of the clues are disguised on historical artifacts and in national monuments. At one point in the movie, they discover that a clue was written on the back of the Declaration of Independence. However, having been written in special ink, they can only see it properly with one special pair of eyeglasses. The glasses have three different-colored lenses that, when used in the right order, allows the viewer to read the message. It is similar to our discipleship; we need all of the lenses to see the truth with clarity.

As church leaders, we encourage you to see the whole picture of transformation, to see discipleship through all three lenses of truth. If you fail to view discipleship through all three lenses, you and the people you serve will not see the totality of transformation. Your people must first and constantly live in the truth of the gospel, so let's begin there.

4

The Gospel Lens

Reminding ourselves of the gospel is the most important daily habit we can possess.
—C. J. Mahaney[1]

BACK IN THE DAY when the church Eric served in Miami still offered "The South Florida Easter Pageant," an elaborate presentation depicting the life, death, and resurrection of Jesus, a couple approached him with concerns about "the performance." They wanted to know if "the show was going to be different." Not sure what they meant, he asked for clarification.

"Well," they continued, "we have been Christians for a long time, and the last few years it has been the same show, and we were hoping it would be, well, you know . . . um, different."

Eric said, "He still rises from the dead. I hope that does not disappoint you."

The couple wrongly viewed the message of Jesus' life, death, and resurrection as elementary, as something they graduated from years ago. In their minds they needed something more, something new and fresh, something "different." In essence they wanted something more advanced.

But the last thing the couple needed was a different story. To the contrary they needed a better understanding of the story they inadvertently had dismissed as no longer applicable to their lives.

Sadly they are not alone in their thinking. Many Christians think the gospel was absolutely essential for justification (declared righteous by Christ) but has little to do with sanctification (the process of becoming more holy). The message often subtly communicated in churches is that the gospel is for unbelievers. Logically believers need more. Nothing could be further from the truth.

If people in our churches graduate from the gospel, they are not advancing to spiritual maturity but rather to lifeless religion, moralistic self-righteousness, or performance-based faith inaccurately called Christian. Only Jesus has the power to melt our hearts; thus there is no transformation apart from the truth of the gospel.

The apostle Paul believed the gospel to be essential for both justification and sanctification. He reminded believers in Corinth about the importance of the gospel.

> Now brothers, I want to clarify for you the gospel I
> proclaimed to you; you received it and have taken your
> stand on it. You are also saved by it, if you hold to the
> message I proclaimed to you—unless you believed for no
> purpose. For I passed on to you as most important what
> I also received: that Christ died for our sins according
> to the Scriptures, that He was buried, that He was raised

on the third day according to the Scriptures, and that
He appeared to Cephas, then to the Twelve. Then He
appeared to over 500 brothers at one time, most of them
are still alive, but some have fallen asleep. Then He
appeared to James, then to all the apostles. Last of all, as
to one abnormally born, He also appeared to me. (1 Cor.
15:1–8)

The apostle says, "You have taken your stand on the gospel"
because he trusts the sufficiency of the gospel for spiritual maturation and transformation. When viewing discipleship through the
lens of the gospel, the goal is to apply the gospel to all of life, to
continually stand on the gospel as the gospel impacts everything.

The gospel impacts everything, but not everything is the
gospel.

While we are grateful for the return to the gospel, the essence
of the Christian faith, it is now hip to call anything and everything
"the gospel." The word *gospel* has often become the junk drawer for
many things that are not the gospel;[2] therefore, to see discipleship
clearly through the lens of the gospel, we must be reminded what
the gospel actually is.

Clarifying the Gospel

Gospel is the Greek word *evangelion*, and it means "good
news." Thus, the gospel is fundamentally news and not advice.
Advice is typically counsel about something that has not yet
happened and requires the listener to do something. *Dress like
this for the date. Ask these questions in the interview. Use this type
of fertilizer on the lawn.* We are bombarded daily with advice on a
myriad of subjects.

News, however, is inherently different. News is a report about a definitive event that has already happened. The listener cannot impact the outcome of the event. The listener simply responds to what has already been done.

The gospel is good news.

Since the advent of twenty-four-hour, around-the-clock news channels, we often confuse news and advice. Stories about news and stories about advice are interspersed in the same programs. A news story about a world event may be followed by advice on how to cut personal expenses in a recession or what colors to avoid wearing during certain months. And since it is all on the news channel, every story gets called "the news." But a lot of what is called news is not actually news. It is just pithy advice.

The same is true in many churches; advice often masquerades as the gospel. Messages filled with advice to help people improve their lives or turn over a new leaf are in contradiction to the nature of the gospel—news we must respond to, not insight we should consider heeding. Church leaders offering advice and calling it gospel will not develop transformed disciples. Worse, they will confuse people as to the true nature and content of the Christian faith. In churches where transformation is most likely to occur, the gospel is prominent and advice diminishes. As believers respond to the Scriptures, transformation takes place.

For weeks after September 11, 2001, all advice ceased on the news channels. There was continual coverage of the events surrounding the terrorist attacks of 9–11. The messengers of the news were convinced of the epic nature of the event and its astounding implications. In the wake of such a life-altering event, the news channels dared not report on something as trivial as advice on portfolio diversification or wardrobe selection. The news rightly dominated.

The good news that Jesus suffered and died in our place for our sin in order that we may freely receive God's righteousness and forgiveness is infinitely more epic, and its dominance in discipleship should accurately reflect that it is "most important."

Snapshot of the Gospel

Entire lifetimes of study on the nature and comprehensiveness of the gospel fall short of its beauty and significance, but we want to offer a simple snapshot. The apostle Paul clearly stated that the gospel brings salvation and is the core message of the Christian faith on which we stand. How does the gospel bring salvation?

The apostle Paul explains why the gospel brings salvation in what most theologians believe to be the central verses in the book of Romans:

> For I am not ashamed of the gospel, because it is God's power for salvation to everyone who believes, first to the Jew, and also to the Greek. For in it God's righteousness is revealed from faith to faith, just as it is written: The righteous will live by faith. (Rom. 1:16–17)

In the gospel God's righteousness is revealed. The snapshot of the gospel is God's righteousness freely given to us.

God is infinitely more holy and pure than can ever be imagined, and surpassingly so. As Jonathan Edwards stated, "All things else, with regard to worthiness, importance, and excellence, are perfectly as nothing in comparison to him."[3] His righteousness is beyond our ability to fathom.

> *The snapshot of the gospel is God's righteousness freely given to us.*

Because God is righteous, He demands righteousness. Without perfection and holiness we are unable to be with Him, unable to receive eternal life. No matter what spiritual advice we follow, because of our sin, we are incapable of making ourselves worthy to approach Him. In fact, even our good deeds fall woefully short of His holiness. Even our goodness is filthy rags compared to His perfection (Isa. 64:6).

As a young monk, Martin Luther hated Romans 1:17 because of the phrase, "God's righteousness." He dreaded the phrase because he knew no matter how hard he tried he could not attain the righteousness of God. At a young age Luther attempted to earn God's righteousness. He legislated his own morality with rules, regulations, and religious advice. And he grew increasingly more frustrated because the laws he set for himself and the strenuous religious pursuits never delivered righteousness to him. His attempts only increased his understanding of his sinfulness and his hatred for "God's righteousness" because he knew it was farther from his grasp than when he first began.

But God in His great mercy used Romans 1:17 to bring the truth of the gospel to Luther's heart. After studying the verse day and night, Luther was awakened to the beauty of the gospel:

> At last, by the mercy of God, mediating day and night, I gave heed to the context of the words. There I began to understand the righteousness of God is righteousness with which the merciful God justifies us by faith. . . . Here I felt that I was altogether born again and had entered paradise itself through open gates.[4]

God requires righteousness; and in His grace, through the sacrifice of Jesus, He freely gives it to all who repent and trust Him. Our righteous God gives His righteousness in exchange for the sinfulness of sinful people. Because of his understanding of this incredible truth, Luther coined the theological phrase that should melt our hearts—"a blessed exchange."

> Faith unites the soul with Christ as a spouse with her husband. Everything which Christ has becomes the property of the believing soul; everything which the soul has becomes the property of the Christ. Christ possesses all blessings and eternal life: they are thenceforward the property of the soul. The soul has all the iniquities and sins: they become thenceforward the property of Christ. It is then a blessed exchange commences.[5]

The Great Exchange

Kyle McDonald is a Canadian who became famous for an amazing story. He was without a job, essentially had no money, and his girlfriend was floating his rent. Yet he wanted to own a house.

All he had was one red paper clip. He decided to offer the red paper clip on Craigslist in exchange for something else, anything else. A girl in Vancouver offered him a fish pen in exchange for his paper clip. He traded the fish pen for a doorknob and the door-knob for a camping stove, the camping stove for a generator, then the generator for a neon sign. Kyle continued his online exchanges (fourteen in all) and landed a small acting job that he exchanged for a house. He began with one red paper clip and, after fourteen exchanges, received a house.[6]

A paper clip for a house.

That is a great exchange, but it still pales in comparison to what we have received.

All we had to offer God was our sin, much less desirable than a paper clip. "The only thing of my own which I can contribute to my own redemption is the sin from which I need to be redeemed."[7] The only thing we bring to the table is our sin, but He graciously takes it from us. And amazingly in exchange, He gives us all His righteousness.

Psalm 32 is an Old Testament celebration of the Great Exchange.

> How joyful is the one whose transgression is forgiven,
> whose sin is covered! How joyful is the man the LORD
> does not charge with sin and in whose spirit is no deceit!
> When I kept silent, my bones became brittle from my
> groaning all day long. For day and night Your hand
> was heavy on me; my strength was drained as in the
> summer's heat. Then I acknowledged my sin to You and
> did not conceal my iniquity. I said, "I will confess my
> transgressions to the LORD," and You took away the guilt
> of my sin. (Ps. 32:1–5)

Psalm 32 is the sequel to Psalm 51, which we looked at earlier. In 2 Samuel 11–12 we found the story of David's sin with Bathsheba, the elaborate cover-up, her husband's death and the confrontation with the prophet Nathan. The forgiveness and restoration David sought with God is recorded in Psalm 51. And in Psalm 32 he celebrates the forgiveness that has been joyfully realized. His shame has been exchanged for God's joy.

Augustine (a leader of the church in the fourth and fifth centuries) loved the psalm so much that he had it inscribed on the wall next to his deathbed so he could mediate on the beauty of the gospel. Though we may not inscribe the words on the wall, mediating on the reality of the "great exchange" is essential for transformational discipleship.

The same three Hebrew words used in Psalm 51 revealing the comprehensive nature of sin are used in Psalm 32. But there are also three Hebrew words used to show the comprehensive nature of forgiveness. The three words for forgiveness trump the three words for sin, revealing that our forgiveness is even deeper than our sin. Charles Spurgeon wrote of this psalm that "the trinity of grace conquers the trinity of sin."[8]

Our carrying is exchanged with His carrying away.

When David carried his own sin, he was miserable. He was plagued with guilt, burdened with the pain of his choices, and filled with anguish because he was not in close communion with God. His sin hijacked the abundant life that is offered to those of us who know God. His joy and peace in God were drained because of what he was carrying (v. 4).

Part of David's misery came from God. Because David belonged to God, God did not allow David to be satisfied in his sin. Out of loving discipline to woo David back to Himself, God placed His heavy hand on David's life.

In His great mercy God carried away all of David's sin and guilt. David's carrying of his sin and shame was exchanged for God's carrying away his sin and shame. The word for "forgiven" in verse 1 is the Hebrew word *naw-saw*, and it means "to lift or carry away." When God forgives us, He carries away our sins and separates them infinitely from us. In our interviews Leonard Sweet reflected on this same idea. He said, "The life that God has prepared for all of us who live in this reality of what it means that we aren't called to live our life alone. That Jesus wants to live His resurrection life in and through us." We are given so much when we have nothing to offer in return.

Our covering is exchanged with His covering.

Like many of us, David initially attempted to hide his sin. Like a dog that foolishly thinks kicking some grass backwards will cover up his mess, David thought that with Bathsheba's husband dead and Bathsheba now as his wife, his sin was covered. But he was wrong, as God sees everything. His covering was woefully insufficient. When David finally gave up the futile attempt to cover his own sin, God stepped in with His covering. The word for "covered" in verse 1 is the Hebrew word *kaw-saw*, and it means much more than covering your bed with a sheet or your pancakes with syrup. *Kaw-saw* means "to hide without any possibility of finding, to bury out of sight forever." He does not merely sprinkle His grace on top of our sin. He covers our sin completely.

> *He does not merely sprinkle His grace on top of our sin.*

Humanity has always attempted to cover sins. When Adam and Eve disobeyed God, they realized they were naked and attempted to cover themselves with fig leaves. Their covering was insufficient. So God, in His mercy, fashioned clothes for them in the garden of Eden by sacrificing an animal and using its skin. Immediately after the first sin came the first sacrifice, which foreshadows the all-sufficient sacrifice of Jesus.

Our recounting is exchanged with His not counting.

David recounted and confessed his sins to God, and God did not count David's sins against him. The Hebrew phase for "does not count" or "does not charge" is *lo-chasab,* and it means there is absolutely no counting, remembering, or reckoning of sin. Sin is wiped away. The debt is paid. The counting of our sins and the just charge against us because of our sin has completely and utterly ceased.

The apostle Paul quotes Psalm 32 in the book of Romans to show that our sin is not counted because the Lord credits His righteousness to us. Our sin is not counted because all of His righteousness is counted (Rom. 4:5–8).

My (Eric's) oldest daughter Eden spent some time at the house of a family we respect. She came home wanting to copy a practice she observed at their house. She wanted to have a chart on the refrigerator where every time she obeyed we would put a sticker on her chart.

These parents do a great job of connecting their kids' behavior to the heart, but Eden was not getting it. She would do something she deemed as "good" or "sweet" and receive a sticker in return.

And then hit her sister with a toy.

We quickly abandoned the chart and sticker strategy, but after Eden went to bed, we discussed how to use the chart to teach her the gospel. We are convinced that only God can change her heart, and we want to be offensive parents aiming at heart transformation and not merely behavior modification. So I sat at the table and filled the entire chart with the stickers.

When Eden woke up, we handed her the chart, and all the spaces were filled with stickers. She was shocked. Her face lit up with awe and anticipation.

"Eden, Daddy filled in all the stickers for you because he loves you. I want you to obey me because I love you and you love me. I don't want you to obey me to get a sticker. I want you to obey me because I love you. I filled in your stickers for you."

"Do I still get a prize?" was her response.

"Yes. Yes you do. But I want you to know that this is what Jesus does for us. We can never get enough stickers. Daddy can never be good enough to get enough stickers. But Jesus fills them in for us."

We talked about the stickers the entire trip to the store for a Barbie Island Princess. By God's grace her heart will be melted by this truth. By God's grace our hearts are still melted by this truth. He has given us all His stickers, all His righteousness; therefore, there is no charge against us. No more counting.

David's celebration of the great exchange ultimately points to the cross. Jesus can carry away our sin because He carried the cross. He can cover our sin because His blood is the atoning (covering) sacrifice. He does not count our sin because all our sin was counted on Him on the cross.

> *Constant awe and appreciation of the gospel leads to a transformed disciple.*

Transformational discipleship occurs when we view the process through the lens of the gospel. By the gospel and the whole counsel of God in the Scriptures, we come to understand how God works for us and in us. Constant awe and appreciation of the gospel leads to a transformed disciple.

Gospel-Driven Awe

In reference to the gospel of our salvation, the apostle Peter wrote:

> Concerning this salvation, the prophets who prophesied about the grace that would come to you searched and carefully investigated. They inquired into what time or what circumstances the Spirit of Christ within them was indicating when He testified in advance to the messianic

sufferings and the glories that would follow. It was
revealed to them that they were not serving themselves
but you. These things have now been announced to you
through those who preached the gospel to you by the
Holy Spirit sent from heaven. Angels desire to look into
these things. (1 Pet. 1:10–12)

Three groups related to the gospel are mentioned in this passage: prophets, apostles, and angels. The prophets were those who
foretold the gospel. Peter paints the picture that as they wrote
down the prophecies about Christ, they would step back from
their writing with an expectant and excited heart, thrilled yet overwhelmed with knowledge too great to comprehend. They searched
Scriptures trying to understand what they wrote as the gospel was
more beautiful and amazing than they could grasp. The apostles
witnessed the work of Christ in the first century. The apostles went
on to declare the gospel after the prophecies were fulfilled in Jesus.

Then there are the angels. They "desire to look into these
things."

The word for "desire" in the original language speaks of having a desire that is not easily satisfied. The word for "look" in the
original language means to stoop down. The angels have this overwhelming and unquenchable desire to stoop down and look into
the gospel.

But didn't they have front-row seats? Weren't they deeply
involved in the apex of the gospel narrative—Christ entering our
world on a rescue mission?

For example, in Luke 1 an angel tells Mary that she is the one
who has been chosen to give birth to the Christ. Understandably
Mary's whole "Holy Spirit story" did not make a lot of sense to
Joseph, so in Matthew 1 an angel comes to Joseph with the same

news. Angels delivered the news to Mary and Joseph, yet they desire to look into these things?

In Luke 2, right after Jesus was born, an angel of the Lord stood before a group of shepherds who were watching their sheep at night. The angel made the first birth announcement and invited others to go and worship Him, yet they desire to look into these things?

In Matthew 2, weeks after Mary gave birth to Jesus, the Child was in grave danger. Herod was threatened by the excitement of a new King being born and has decided that all males born in Bethlehem should be killed. But an angel of the Lord warned Joseph in a dream to flee Bethlehem. Angels were a part of protecting the child and ensuring that Christ would grow up and take the sins of the world upon Himself. Later, after an intense season of testing in the wilderness, angels ministered to Jesus (Matt. 4). Yet they desire to look into these things?

Angels are eternal beings that forever enjoy the presence of God. What did they miss that stirs such a longing in them?

Angels know all about the gospel, but they do not know the gospel. They have never experienced gospel transformation because they have never needed to be transformed. Unlike believers, angels have never been rescued and do not know the gratitude of being rescued by Jesus. And, unlike believers, angels have never been restored. They don't fully understand the joy that comes when Jesus transforms brokenness into wholeness.

Angels are filled with awe for the gospel; how much more should those who have experienced it? When we are overwhelmed with awe for Jesus and His righteousness freely given to us, we are filled with the motivation to live a godly life in Christ Jesus. We obey because our hearts are melted by the devastatingly refreshing truth of the gospel. The reminder of the gospel motivates us to live out the transformation Christ has already brought to us.

Living Out the Gospel

In the Transformational Discipleship (TD) research, the issue of biblical engagement was a key attribute in discipleship. As believers grow in their faith, they should have a deeper longing to encounter biblical truth. When believers are willing to place their lives on a collision course with God's Word, then transformation can occur. When faced with the statement, "I desire to please and honor Jesus in all that I do," 90 percent of believers agree (64 percent strongly agree, and 26 percent agree somewhat). Because of the gospel, the growing believer responds with a deep gratitude resulting in an obedient life.

A majority of believers also agreed with the statement, "Throughout the day I find myself thinking about biblical truths" (59 percent either strongly or somewhat agreed strongly). Seeing life through the lens of Scripture and transformational discipleship go hand in hand. The study also looked into the actions that can positively impact a Christian's maturity. The first two are simple: read and study the Bible. The most basic forms of engagement with God's Word and His gospel stand out if we hope to see people move to the TSS. The study also revealed that confessing sin to God, choosing to obey His Word no matter the personal cost, and reading other material that enhances our biblical knowledge are actions believers can take to mature.

Churches that constantly apply the gospel to people's hearts will see the inner transformation only God can bring. These churches understand that the gospel is the motivation for all of the Christian life. Viewing discipleship through the lens of the gospel causes leaders to see the embedded connections between the gospel and maturity.

Impacts Everything

Seeing discipleship through the lens of the gospel means applying the gospel to all of life, believing transformation occurs when disciples center their lives on the gospel. The gospel is sufficient; it is enough. It is relevant. It is not merely the foundational curriculum for a disciple but the overarching curriculum. Tim Keller writes:

> The Christian life is a process of renewing every dimension of our life—spiritual, psychological, corporate, social—by thinking, hoping, and living out the ramifications or the gospel. The gospel is to be applied to every area of thinking, feeling, relating, working and behaving.[9]

Instead of approaching discipleship as something beyond the gospel, apply the gospel to every area of life. Instead of giving advice about marriage, show the implications of the gospel on marriage. Instead of offering parenting insight, show how the gospel impacts parenting. Instead of looking for a new angle on giving and stewardship challenges, bring people to the gospel. Instead of tapping into the altruistic movements in society as motivation for serving, show how the gospel is the impetus for serving. And mission, and obedience, and forgiveness, and hospitality, and . . .

The gospel impacts everything.

> *The gospel is sufficient; it is enough.*

Here are a few examples of the gospel's impacting aspects of a disciple's life, aspects of a disciple's life that are commonly taught in churches.

Gospel and Marriage

In his letter to the Ephesian church, the apostle Paul specifically addressed marriage. In Ephesus men typically viewed women as property, not as someone who should be loved and cherished. They often treated marriage as a business transaction for the sake of social appearances, thus they sought sexual gratification outside their marriage. While the cultural norms in Ephesus stood in stark contrast to God's law, the apostle Paul never addressed them. Instead he simply told men to reflect on God's great love for them as the motivation for their marriages.

> Husbands, love your wives, just as Christ loved the
> church and gave Himself for her to make her holy,
> cleansing her with the washing of water by the word.
> (Eph. 5:25–26)

Paul essentially said, "Guys, let your hearts be melted by Christ's pursuit of you. He loved you when you were cold to Him. He gave everything up to cleanse you. If you are having a difficult time loving and pursuing your spouse, come back to the gospel and repent. Love your spouse as Christ loved you. Serve your spouse as He served you."

Often our first impulse is to give marital advice. Who knows? Maybe some of the Ephesians expected Paul to rattle some helpful marriage principles or recommend a conference—which can be good things. But he did neither. He simply reminded men and women of the gospel and showed them how the gospel impacts marriage. Quoting the book of Genesis, Paul showed that marriage is actually a beautiful reflection of the gospel:

> For this reason a man will leave his father and mother and be joined to his wife, and the two will become one flesh. This mystery is profound, but I am talking about Christ and the church. (Eph. 5:31–32)

"Mystery" in the text does not mean something too deep or complex to understand, rather something that was hidden in the Old Testament that has now been revealed. Paul showed that under the Old Covenant the union between man and woman pointed to something more profound than the marriage itself, and what marriage pointed to was a mystery until Christ was revealed. Marriage is a metaphor and a shadow of the eternal marriage God has with His people.

A disciple's marriage points to the ultimate marriage and therefore has profound significance. This is why God hates divorce so much. Divorce is a massive contradiction of the gospel and an inaccurate reflection on the eternal marriage between God and His people. He will never divorce His bride, will never forsake her, and will never cheat on her. Thus, as we prioritize the gospel in our lives and marriages, our relationship with God and our spouse will deepen.

Viewing discipleship through the lens of the gospel will also impact how church leaders challenge and encourage marriages. Church leaders will not rush to offer more marriage personality studies, events for couples, or facilitated date nights but will seek to ground couples in the gospel.

Gospel and Worship

Worship is the most appropriate response to the gospel. When challenging people to worship, both corporately and personally, churches that view discipleship through the gospel lens articulate that attitude. When God gave the Ten Commandments to His people, He first reminded them of the freedom He graciously gave them.

> I am the LORD your God, who brought you out of the
> land of Egypt, out of the place of slavery. Do not have
> other gods besides Me. (Exod. 20:2–3)

The first commandment instructs us to worship only God, to have nothing else that captures our hearts. Prior to giving the command, God reminds the people that He rescued them from Egyptian captivity. He has rescued us from the captivity of our sin, and we shall have no other god before Him. The foundation for worship is the gospel. As the psalmist commands us in Psalm 150, we should offer Him passionate praise because of His powerful acts on our behalf (v. 2).

The implications are numerous, but churches viewing worship through the lens of the gospel select songs that remind the people of the

> **The foundation for worship is the gospel.**

gospel and call for a response because of the gospel. Tradition or styles are not the starting point in song selection, but the gospel is. Instead of thinly veiled songs that could easily be sung to a boyfriend or girlfriend, songs that clearly point to Jesus are selected. While you can gaze into the eyes of anyone or have anyone embrace you, only God gives you His righteousness and rids you of all your sin.

Gospel and Giving

Church leaders are bombarded with advice on "raising capital," "developing donors," "cultivating generosity," and "teaching stewardship." With giving as a clear mark of spiritual health, the church needs resources to be all she should be in the community where God has placed her. If the apostle Paul were at the table hearing church leaders bemoan the lack of giving in their churches, he would probably say, "The people must have forgotten the gospel or not truly embraced it." Paul emphasized the gospel in his appeal for believers to be generous in giving:

> Now as you excel in everything—faith, speech,
> knowledge, and in all diligence, and in your love for
> us—excel also in this grace. I am not saying this as a
> command. Rather, by means of the diligence of others, I
> am testing the genuineness of your love. For you know
> the grace of our Lord Jesus Christ: Though He was rich,
> for your sake He became poor, so that by His poverty you
> might become rich. (2 Cor. 8:7–9)

Leaders who view discipleship through the lens of the gospel apply the gospel to finances by constantly reminding people of God's great generosity. He who was rich became more to make us rich, eternally. When the "per capita" giving drops in a church, these leaders are more concerned with the lack of gospel internalization in their people than the budget implications.

Gospel and Serving

Jesus motivated His disciples to serve people by connecting His challenge for them to serve with the reality that He served them first. At the Last Supper, Jesus washed the feet of His disciples and said to them:

> So if I, your Lord and Teacher, have washed your feet,
> you also ought to wash one another's feet. For I have

given you an example that you also should do just as I
have done for you. (John 13:14–15)

Viewing discipleship through the lens of the gospel impacts
how church leaders communicate the value of serving to the
people they lead. Instead of promoting volunteer opportunities
as opportunities to "do good," which can drift into moralistic
attempts to earn God's favor, people are reminded of the gospel
and challenged to "serve because Christ has served you."

Gospel and the Poor

The apostle Paul reminded the Corinthian Christians of their
status when Christ called them to Himself.

Brothers, consider your calling: Not many are wise from
a human perspective, not many powerful, not many of
noble birth. Instead, God has chosen what is foolish
in the world to shame the wise, and God has chosen
what is weak in the world to shame the strong. God has
chosen what is insignificant and despised in the world—
what is viewed as nothing—to bring to nothing what is
viewed as something, so that no one can boast in His
presence. (1 Cor. 1:26–29)

Before a holy God, all of us were poor. No one was worthy, yet
God in His great love pursued us. He did not pursue us as a coach
pursues "A-level players" for a team or an executive recruits "tens"
for his organization. He pursued us when we were spiritually
ruined. We were poor and desolate of soul. In fact, the gospel is
only for the poor—those who realize they are spiritually poor and
absolutely bankrupt before God.

We rejoice for those believers and churches impacting cities, serving the poor, and defending those accosted by injustice. Churches who view discipleship through the lens of the gospel understand that ministry to the underresourced and hurting flows from a commitment to the mission of God. The embrace of the gospel will cause us to embrace more deeply its ministry of reconciliation. Thus, we will not fall prey to the dangers of a bland "social gospel" that merely feeds the body. Rather, churches will embrace the gospel that cares for the soul in need of redemption and the city in need of restoration. Leaders who see through the gospel lens remind people how God rescued them in their spiritual poverty and connect the beauty of that reality to serving the underresourced.

Gospel and Others

Throughout the Scriptures numerous commands are given for how believers are to treat one another. The foundation for these commands, whether explicitly stated or implicitly implied through the grand narrative of the text, is the gospel.

> Therefore accept one another, just as the Messiah also accepted you, to the glory of God. (Rom. 15:7)

> And be kind and compassionate to one another, forgiving one another, just as God also forgave you in Christ. (Eph. 4:32)

> Just as I have loved you, you must also love one another. (John 13:34)

Leaders who view discipleship through the lens of the gospel don't only hold Christ as the standard for acceptance, forgiveness, and love—though that is true and essential to remind people of their need for His grace—they also remind people of the greatness of God's love, acceptance, and forgiveness expressed toward them. As people are increasingly grateful for the truth of the gospel, their love, forgiveness, and acceptance of others will increase as well. A gospel-lens leader views unfriendliness in a church as a gospel-integration issue and assumes responsibility to remind people of the gospel and its implications.

Transformation happens when believers boldly embrace what Christ does through the gospel. Furthermore, believers should be willing to go public with the changes. The TD research revealed that 72 percent disagreed with the statement, "Many people who know me are not aware that I am a Christian" (37 percent strongly and 35 percent somewhat). Half of the believers disagreed some-what or strongly with the statement, "Spiritual matters do not tend to come up as a normal part of my daily conversations with other Christians." The implication is that discussions about and living out the implications of the gospel is seen as normal for believers.

Gospel and Holiness

Before the apostle Paul challenged believers in Romans 6:12 to "not let sin reign in their bodies," he reminded them of the gospel and connected the imperative of personal holiness to the death, burial, and resurrection of Jesus. Paul's point was, "Your sin was crucified and buried with Christ. Why would you want to live in it any longer?"

> What should we say then? Should we continue in sin so
> that grace may multiply? Absolutely not! How can we
> who died to sin still live in it? Or are you unaware that all
> of us who were baptized into Christ Jesus were baptized
> into His death? Therefore we were buried with Him

by baptism into death, in order that, just as Christ was raised from the dead by the glory of the Father, so we too may walk in a new way of life. (Rom. 6:1–4)

The implications continue endlessly because the implications of the life, death, burial, and resurrection of Jesus are endless. The apostle John closed his Gospel account with this statement about Jesus:

And there are also many other things that Jesus did, which, if they were written one by one, I suppose not even the world itself could contain the books that would be written. (John 21:25)

There is more to the life of Jesus than could be recorded within the pages of the Bible. But the core of the message—the gospel—has been perfectly communicated to us. It is the content of God's mission and the message encapsulated in Jesus' ministry. For us it is the lens through which we understand and live out our faith.

5
The Identity Lens

People need to be reminded more than instructed.
—C. S. Lewis

JANE ELLIOT BECAME FAMOUS for a learning exercise she developed with her elementary students more than thirty years ago. When students in an all-white town in rural Iowa were confused about the meanings of racism, bigotry, and discrimination following the assassination of Dr. Martin Luther King, Jane came to class prepared to guide her students through a memorable learning experience.

She walked into class and declared that brown-eyed students were smarter than the blue-eyed students. The students with brown eyes were moved to the front of the classroom, given extra time at recess, and afforded the favor of their teacher. The blue-eyed students were given special collars to wear so that everyone could see from a distance that they were inferior. The following day Jane announced to the class that she was mistaken; actually the blue-eyed students were superior to the brown-eyed students. The blue-eyed students ripped off the collars with joy.

The simple experiment revealed that the students lived out of their declared identity. On the days when students wore the collars as symbols of their inferiority, they described feelings of sadness and their academic performance was also affected. For example, when the blue-eyed students wore the collars, they needed 5.5 minutes to complete a reading exercise. When the students were declared to be the smartest students and free from the dreaded collars, they were filled with confidence and completed the reading exercise in 2.5 minutes.

Their understanding of their identity impacted how they lived.

In the early 1970s psychology professor Philip Zimbardo led a team of scientists from Stanford University in a controversial experiment that is still referenced today both in academic circles and pop culture. The team built a mock prison in the basement of the university's psychology department and placed advertisements in the local papers looking for volunteers. They selected twenty-four people to participate, choosing the ones who appeared to be the most emotionally stable and healthy.

Half of the participants were randomly selected to be prison guards. They were given military-style guard uniforms and dark glasses and were told their responsibility was to keep order. The others became the prisoners. They were arrested in their homes, cuffed, brought to a real police station, fingerprinted, and blindfolded for the trip to the mock prison. They wore prison clothes with numbers on the front and back of the clothing and were only allowed to refer to themselves and others by their numbers.

The experiment quickly spiraled out of control. The guards transformed into overly aggressive alpha males who sought to humiliate the others. Four of the prisoners were pulled from the experiment early because of emotional breakdowns including extreme depression, crying, rage, and anxiety. The experiment was intended to last two weeks, but Zimbardo shut it down after six days. For both the guards and the prisoners, understanding their identity deeply impacted their thinking, attitude, and behavior.

> *Our understanding of our identity impacts how we live.*

Our understanding of our identity impacts how we live.

Transformational discipleship results in transformed living by believers who understand and live out their new God-given identity.

Becoming Who We Are

Salvation begins with justification as Christ declares His own righteous and ends with glorification when believers enjoy eternity without the presence of sin. The process between the two is sanctification. Sanctification is the process of being made holy by the One who has declared us holy and walking in newness of life because He has made us new. God is perfecting those He has already declared perfect and continually purifies those He has already made pure through Christ (Heb. 10:14).

While, for the believer, justification is a past event and glorification is a future event, sanctification is ongoing and continual. It is happening right now. Sanctification is the process of becoming who we already are. It is about living out our identity.

I (Philip) have two sons, and when my wife Angie was pregnant, we went through the universal ritual of picking out names. The names we chose have particular significance. For our first son, we chose the name Andrew Timothy, which, when combined, means "the strong one who honors God." For our second son we chose Christopher Sage; the names combined mean "the strong one with Christ inside."

When they were infants, the meanings were, well, meaningless because my boys had no way of fulfilling their identity. Now they have come to trust Christ personally and are teenagers. As they grow, my wife and I hope to guide them toward living out the meaning of their names. We want them to have a strong identity.

> *Leaders remind people of who they are in Christ.*

God has graciously given us a new identity, and sanctification is the process of becoming what God has already declared us to be. God commands us to live out our calling, to live in response to the great identity He has given (Eph. 4:1; Phil. 3:16). As believers understand their identity, they are empowered by God to flesh out their identity in everyday life.

Leaders who view discipleship through the lens of identity encourage and train people to live in response to the great identity God has given. Instead of beginning with behavior, leaders remind people of who they are in Christ. They connect the commands of God to the identity He secures for His followers, presenting obedience as the overflow of understanding and living the new nature Christ has given. As Earl Creps said in our discipleship interviews, "Jesus is not a food additive. He doesn't come to improve your life. He's come to be your life."

Pastor Peter's Challenge

The apostle Peter viewed discipleship, in part, through the lens of identity in Christ. When he wrote the epistle of 1 Peter, he was writing a group of Christians who were struggling with how to live in the world as they were experiencing intense persecution. The root of the hostility toward them was the fire that burned Rome to the ground. The Roman culture was devastated as careers were lost, homes were burned, and families were ripped apart.

As often occurs when a national tragedy strikes, the Roman citizens wanted to blame someone. Initially the Romans believed that Nero, the Roman emperor, had set fire to his own city. He was suspected of the unthinkable act because of his insatiable desire to build new things.

Nero responded to the anger and suspicion by shifting the blame and hatred toward Christians. He accused Christians of setting fire to the city, and great hostility broke out against the Christians throughout the Roman Empire. Because Christians were spread and dispersed, Peter wrote a letter to encourage them to continue in the faith. He reminded them of their new identity and challenged them to live accordingly.

> But you are a chosen race, a royal priesthood, a holy nation, a people for His possession, so that you may proclaim the praises of the One who called you out of darkness into His marvelous light. Once you were not a people, but now you are God's people; you had not received mercy, but now you have received mercy. Dear friends, I urge you as strangers and temporary residents to abstain from fleshly desires that war against you. Conduct yourselves honorably among the Gentiles, so that in a case where they speak against you as those who do what is evil, they will, by observing your good works, glorify God on the day of visitation. (1 Pet. 2:9–12)

In a few short sentences Peter reminds people they are chosen, priests, holy, God's possession, and strangers in this world. Peter urges these believers (and us) to proclaim God's praises, live pure, and engage nonbelievers with integrity. But notice how he connects the commands to their new identity. He connects their sanctification (living out their faith) to their justification (who Christ has declared them to be).

Unfortunately the self-help movement has hijacked critical teaching on our identity in Christ. Many leaders have overreacted to the narcissism of the Christianized self-help section of Barnes and Noble by refusing to touch the identity lens. Sadly, the result is that many Christians fail to realize the greatness of their identity.

The end result of understanding our identity is not looking in the mirror and telling ourselves how awesome we are. In fact, our new identity is ultimately not about us. Our identity is from God and results in God's being glorified. As Peter highlighted, the end result of understanding our identity is that Christ is proclaimed. When we really understand who God has made us to be, the automatic response is to declare how great God is. Not how great we are.

> *Our new identity is ultimately not about us.*

Living Our Identity

Our identity in Christ necessitates rejecting an identity built on selfish desires. In the TD research, believers consistently showed that they know this to be the case. When asked about denying selfish impulses, we are glad to see that believers know that being a transformed disciple means living a new life. In response to the statement, "A Christian must learn to deny himself/herself in order to serve Christ," a majority agreed with the statement (36 percent strongly agree, and 28 percent somewhat agree). An even stronger agreement was given to the statement, "I feel sorrow and regret when I realize I have sinned." To this statement, 48 percent strongly agreed, and 38 percent agreed somewhat.

We are glad to see a strong sense among Christians to reject sinful behavior. Transformation is seen when believers are swiftly rejecting that which does not match up with our new identity in Christ. Additionally, decision-making by transformed disciples should be on the basis of choosing God's work in the world even if it is costly to the individual.

Helping people encounter the truth of their identity is vital. As believers understand who they are in Christ, they are motivated to live the reality of their identity. Leaders who see discipleship through the lens of identity are burdened to show people the beautiful ramifications of the identity God brings. They are convinced that a deep hindrance to transformation is seeking satisfaction and fulfillment in a lesser identity, one not found in Christ.

Leaders and churches that view discipleship through the identity lens continually connect the fruit of a transformed life to the identity Christ gives because of the gospel. They are careful not to teach for the fruit of transformation without reminding people of their core identity, the new root God has placed in their lives. Leonard Sweet reminds us: "My fundamental identity is as a follower. As I invite people to follow me, but follow me only as I follow Christ. . . . This is the essence of [my] followership."

Who has Christ declared believers to be (justification)? And how does this impact the daily lives of those we serve (sanctification)?

His Child

The apostle John wrote, "Look at how great a love the Father has given us, that we should be called God's children. And we are!" (1 John 3:1).

The word for "given" in the original language is in the perfect tense indicating that God's love is permanently fixed upon His children. He has not casually placed His love on His children; He is all in. His love is completely and extravagantly lavished on us. And we are not just called children of God—we actually are.

We have all been called names that are not true of who we really are. Just because someone calls the New York Knicks a basketball team does not mean they actually are one. As believers we are not merely *called* children of God, we actually are His children. We don't merely carry a business card claiming to be a child of God. We have more than the title hanging on the door.

God uses the image of adoption throughout Scripture to drive home the point that He intentionally made you His child. The picture of adoption is beautiful, as parents search for a child, sometimes enduring lengthy adoption processes, set their love on a child that was not originally their own, carry the child home, and assume all responsibility for the child. With intentional love God has pursued His own. We were not a "surprise" or an "accident." He was fully prepared to be our Father because He adopted us. The apostle Paul wrote:

> All those led by God's Spirit are God's sons. For you did not receive a spirit of slavery to fall back into fear, but you received the Spirit of adoption, by whom we cry out, "Abba, Father!" The Spirit Himself testifies together with our spirit that we are God's children. (Rom. 8:14–16)

Verse 15 uses the intimate phrase, "Abba, Father"—a phrase that was new and exciting for the first believers to receive Paul's letter. The first believers were Jewish, and Jews never dared to utter the name of God. They would never have referred to Him with an affectionate name like "Father."

Theologians are not sure how Yahweh was pronounced in the Old Testament because there is no record of how people pronounced the proper name of God. There is no record of how people pronounced Yahweh because no one ever did. Even when the Jews wrote the name of God, they would leave out the vowels because they believed His name was too pure for human hands to write.

> **With intentional love God has pursued His own.**

When Jesus came to this earth, He referred to God the Father with the intimate Aramaic term "Abba." This was scandalous because the Jews viewed God as distant, too holy even to mention. Jesus enters culture and refers to God with the intimate term "Father."

But there is one moment in the Gospels where Jesus does not use "Abba" in His reference to God the Father. When Jesus is on the cross, He yells out, "My God, My God, why have You forsaken Me?" In this moment Jesus was being condemned for us, becoming sin for us; thus He could not enjoy the close relationship with Abba. He experienced painful separation from the Father so we can experience joyful connection with Him.

The apostle Paul writes the book of Romans in Greek, but when he says, we cry "Abba, Father," he grabs the Aramaic word "Abba" that Jesus used. He is saying we now have the same relationship with God the Father that Jesus enjoyed. He is our Abba, just as He was to Jesus. *Abba* literally means "Daddy." It is a close and affectionate word. So God, who was once perceived as far away and too holy to mention, is our Daddy.

Leaders who see through the identity lens have their hearts melted by this truth, and they connect the new identity of being His child with the commands to trust Him and obey Him as a child trusts and obeys His father. Jesus used children as object lessons of true faith. He longs for His own to trust and obey Him like a son or daughter who is grateful for the provision and care of Daddy.

We can use this affectionate term with God because the Holy Spirit has drawn us into a relationship with Him. It is a portion of the passage that should not be overlooked. Paul wrote that we are "led by God's Spirit" (Rom. 8:14) to become His children and thus "coheirs with Christ" (v. 17). The identity we have in Christ is a work done exclusively by God on our behalf. Just as an orphan child does not go out into the suburbs to seek a new family, we do not seek our way into God's kingdom. Rather, the Spirit seeks us out and then transforms our lives by the power of the gospel.

In leading people to live out their identity as disciples, we should feel a consistent humility because we have been sought rather than living as the seeker. Even as a disciple, a member of God's family, we are still on the receiving end of the seeking by God's Spirit.

As you seek to disciple people for transformation, remind them to connect the commands for obedience to the special relationship they have with the Father. Use the reality of their adoption to drive up gratitude that results in obedience. Apply the truth of the intimacy of a relationship with Abba to the hearts of those you disciple.

His Priest

When Peter told believers they were a "royal priesthood" (1 Pet. 2:9), he was reminding them of a sacred and special facet of their identity. They were born into a culture familiar with the

Jewish sacrificial system where once a year the high priest, and only the high priest, would enter the most holy place in the temple and encounter the presence of God.

Only one person could enter the presence of God in the most holy place until Christ changed everything. During the days of the tabernacle and the temple, the high priest would sacrifice an animal on the bronze altar in the outer court of the temple. He could not enter the presence of God without a sacrifice. When Jesus placed Himself on the cross, He was placing Himself on the sacrificial altar for an all-sufficient sacrifice.

It is no coincidence that God sent His Son to die during a time in history when death by crucifixion was the norm. The death had to be bloody because "without the shedding of blood there is no forgiveness" of sins (Heb. 9:22). It is also no coincidence that Jesus was crucified during the Jewish Passover celebration when lambs were being sacrificed. Jesus "is the Lamb of God, who takes away the sin of the world" (John 1:29).

In the temple a curtain separated the most holy place from the rest of the temple. From the rest of the world.

From you.

This curtain separated us from God. We could not peer behind the curtain. We could not go behind the veil. We could not go where the high priest could go. The curtain was a constant reminder that the presence of God was inaccessible. But when Christ died, a new and living way opened for us. As He was breathing His last breath on the cross, a miraculous event occurred . . .

> Jesus shouted again with a loud voice and gave up His spirit. Suddenly, the curtain of the sanctuary was split in two from top to bottom; the earth quaked and the rocks were split. (Matt. 27:50–51)

As Christ's body was torn, the curtain in the temple was torn. Because Christ's body was torn, the veil was torn. The most holy place became accessible. And we may enter the presence of God. The writer of Hebrews reminds us of the honor we hold as priests of God:

> Therefore, brothers, since we have boldness to enter the sanctuary through the blood of Jesus, by a new and living way He has opened for us through the curtain (that is, His flesh), and since we have a great high priest over the house of God, let us draw near with a true heart in full assurance of faith, our hearts sprinkled clean from an evil conscience and our bodies washed in pure water. (Heb. 10:19–22)

Believers in Christ are priests who may enter the most holy place, who are granted the privilege to spend time with the God of the universe. We may enter His presence with confidence because the curtain, His flesh, was torn for us.

> *The most holy place became accessible.*

Leaders wearing discipleship glasses and peering through the identity lens don't merely preach the priestly functions as commands: pray, represent God to people, love truth, etc. Instead they first remind people they serve of the great identity of being a priest and then connect the exhortations to the identity. The TD research revealed that believers are more likely to readily feel sorrow over sin, confess sin, and take the necessary steps to fix ungodly attitudes. Their minds are fixed on the life before God rather than in fulfilling selfish desires.

Leaders wearing the identity lens who sense a lack of prayer in their people believe they have an "identity deficiency" and they teach the privilege of being His priests. Leaders wearing the identity lens who sense a lack of awe in worship gatherings believe the solution is not teaching people to "do" something but rather reminding them of the great honor of entering the presence of God. Leaders wearing the identity lens who are burdened for the people they serve to spend more time with God don't first rush to a new curriculum; they prayerfully shepherd hearts to be broken with the awesome honor of being God's priest.

His Bride

When many think of discipleship, they think of holy and pure living, and rightly so as *sanctify* literally means "to make holy." Those leaders who view discipleship through the identity lens teach for holiness but are compelled to it with the glorious declaration that God has already made His own people holy.

To describe the depth of our relationship with God, God describes us as His bride (Eph. 5:25). God defines marriage as a covenant relationship where a man and woman become united completely: physically, emotionally, and spiritually. For God marriage unites two people as one (Gen. 2:24). As His bride, we are clothed in His righteousness. He sees us as completely pure because of Jesus (Isa. 61:10), and we will be united with Him forever in what the Bible describes as an eternal marriage (Rev. 19:7).

Leaders who view discipleship through the lens of identity connect the commands to live holy to the reality that God sees us as His bride. Sin is understood as a gross contradiction of the beautiful relationship believers have with Christ. Rather than merely preaching against specific sins, leaders with an identity posture remind believers of who they are and the foolishness of pursing other lovers. In the TD research we discovered that believers want to follow this pattern. In response to the statement,

"I confess my sins and wrongdoings to God and ask forgiveness," 39 percent responded with "every day", and 27 percent responded with "a few times a week."

Because believers are the bride of Christ, sin is cheating on God. To be clearer, sin is cheating on God while wearing the wedding dress He placed on us. To graphically illustrate the unfaithfulness of His people, God instructed one of His prophets, Hosea, to marry a promiscuous wife (Hos. 1:2). When God's people sinned in the Old Testament, He told them they were lying down like a prostitute under every tree (Jer. 2:20).

Adultery always leads to pain, always. The hurt and despair in husbands and wives who are crushed because their spouses pursued intimacy with another lover is immense. Seemingly the pain and regret in those who wandered is equally devastating. Adultery is never worth it; it never delivers on the promise of excitement or intimacy.

Cheating on God is never worth it. Not only do we harm our relationship with Him, but we also find ourselves empty. We regret the choice to stray from Christ because nothing else satisfies like He does. When we choose to seek satisfaction and pleasure in things or people other than God, we commit spiritual adultery by chasing other lovers. And these other lovers cannot satisfy us because they are cracked cisterns. They are incapable of curing our thirst (Jer. 2:13).

Leaders who see through the identity lens have their hearts broken for sin because of the deep violation it is of the sacred and eternal marriage with Christ. They preach, teach, counsel, and shepherd the people they serve to live holy lives because they have been declared holy as the bride of Christ. Rather than issuing a list of "holy principles," they connect the commands for holy living to the reality that believers are the beautiful and holy bride.

An Alien

Another facet of our identity that impacts holy living is the reality that we are aliens in this culture. Peter connected the command to abstain from sin with the identity of being a temporary resident in this world (1 Pet. 2:11–12). Believers are not citizens of the world but citizens of God's kingdom (Phil. 3:20). We are not even dual citizens as if we belong to two kingdoms; we are actually aliens here.

In the original language of Scripture, *alien* literally means "you are someone who lives alongside the people who belong here." As believers we don't really belong, as we are temporary residents in this land because of our faith. Leaders who view discipleship through the lens of identity help the people they serve realize this world is not their ultimate home. When these leaders sense allegiance or attachment to this world, they lovingly remind the people that this world and its pursuits are fleeting.

> We are actually aliens here.

While Peter connects holy living to the identity of an alien, he also emphasizes that personal holiness should be lived out among people who do not know God (1 Pet. 2:12). Those who are growing in the faith live in a way that is visibly different. Sin does not corrupt and destroy the example of believers, and good deeds are visible to the world. Our good deeds will be visible to the world around us. As we live righteously attractive lives, people will take note. People will see our lives, and they will glorify God.

As aliens we do not fully belong here because we have been sent on mission from another kingdom; we are ambassadors.

His Ambassador

Transformed disciples share their faith with others. Leaders who view discipleship through the lens of identity emphasize the new identity Christ has given believers as a foundational reason for evangelism. The apostle Paul wrote:

> Therefore, if anyone is in Christ, he is a new creation; old things have passed away, and look, new things have come. Everything is from God, who reconciled us to Himself through Christ and gave us the ministry of reconciliation: That is, in Christ, God was reconciling the world to Himself, not counting their trespasses against them, and He has committed the message of reconciliation to us. Therefore, we are ambassadors for Christ, certain that God is appealing through us. (2 Cor. 5:17–20)

Paul connected the desire to reconcile others to Christ with both the gospel (Christ reconciled us) and his new identity (we are His ambassadors). An ambassador represents his king and country in a different culture for a specific period of time.

Discipleship leaders who see through the lens of identity remind Christians that they have the honor of being Christ's ambassadors. If they sense a lack of evangelism in their church culture, they crank up an emphasis on reminding people of their fundamental calling as ambassadors. They challenge those they serve to represent Christ in the culture, both in word and deed. When people understand that they are ambassadors, the ordinary becomes sacred, as every moment of each day is an opportunity to represent the King and His kingdom.

His Slave

When Paul, Timothy, and James introduced themselves to churches, they often chose the title "slave" or "bondservant" (Phil. 1:1; Rom. 1:1; James 1:1). The word in the original language is *doulos*, which literally means "a slave who is willingly bound to another." The concept of bondservant was well known in the Jewish culture. Paul, Timothy, and James were using a vivid word to illustrate their fundamental identity as servants of Christ.

In Jewish culture someone who fell on hard times could choose to sell himself as a slave to someone. Many Jews viewed selling themselves as servants as a viable option to provide for their family and survive. This was not slavery as we have imagined slavery because masters treated their servants as family.

God instituted a law among His people that on every seventh year all debts would be completely forgiven. Therefore, slaves would be freed after six years of service. God gave instructions to His people detailing how to free servants who sold themselves into service.

> If your fellow Hebrew, a man or woman, is sold to you
> and serves you six years, you must set him free in the
> seventh year. . . . But if your slave says to you, "I don't
> want to leave you," because he loves you and your family,
> and is well off with you, take an awl and pierce through
> his ear into the door, and he will become your slave for
> life. (Deut. 15:12, 16–17)

Servants were given the option to stay with their master, to continue in the service of the person who bought them. Many chose to stay because life with their master was so much better than life elsewhere. They loved the master and his family and could not imagine living elsewhere. Through a special (yet painful) ceremony, the master and the servant entered into a special relationship, a bond that lasted their entire lives. The servant was marked for life as the willing and grateful servant of his master.

Believers are bondservants of Christ.

Before Christ we were ruined, bankrupt, and without hope. Yet Christ, in His mercy, purchased us with His own blood (1 Pet. 1:18–19). Instead of our being pierced, He took our piercing. He gave us a new life, a home with Him, and a reason to live. The identity of servant should radically impact how a disciple lives.

Leaders who view discipleship through the lens of identity are bent to continually teach believers that their service to Christ and others is the natural response to being a bondservant. They point to the grace of the Master and the privilege of staying and serving. Rather than articulating service as a means to alleviate guilt or boost one's own ego, leaders with the identity lens seek to apply the truth of being a humble and grateful servant to the hearts of those they serve. Church or ministry leaders who see through the identity lens assume that "a low-serving culture" must mean people have forgotten who they are. Rather than first discussing strategies for volunteer engagement, they think first how to remind people of the joy and honor of being a servant of Christ.

Reminding People

Throughout this chapter the emphasis has been kept on the Scriptures. It is where we learn about our identity in Christ. From the research we can see that believers know prioritizing God's authority will lead to growth. Submitting to the work of the Holy Spirit in confession of sin, time spent reading the Word, and interceding for the spiritual status of lost people are all actions believers indicate they can take to grow in their faith. All of these actions come with the understanding that God is the authority in our lives. Only people who gain their identity from God and His work willingly submit themselves to such actions consistently.

As Philip Zimbardo was dismissing some of the mock prisoners from the Stanford basement, he needed to remind them that they were not prisoners, that the scenario was not real. The barrage of accusations from their accusers had taken its toll, and several of the mock prisoners were demoralized.

Just as the guards in the prison experiment bombarded the mock prisoners with messages about their identity, Satan is the accuser who constantly bombards believers with messages. In fact, Satan's name literally means "accuser." Day and night he hurls accusations about those who belong to God (Rev. 12:10). His accusations are lies, while the truth of God is that believers have received a new identity from God for the glory of God.

The accuser tells believers they are guilty. God says there is no condemnation for those who are in Christ (Rom. 8:1). The enemy attempts to convince believers they are trapped in sin. Christ declares you are no longer a slave to sin (Rom. 6:6). While the accuser sends messages about being filthy and unclean, God declares believers have received His righteousness (1 Cor. 1:30). The accuser points to prison walls. God insists believers have been set free (Gal. 5:1).

Those in our churches and in our ministries need to be reminded of their new identity and the resulting freedom. Zimbardo was compelled to tell the mock prisoners that the prison was not real; the nightmare was an experiment. As leaders we must tell believers we disciple the same thing, "You are free. You are forgiven. Live that way."

6
The Discipline Lens

It costs much to obtain this power.
—Adoriam Judson Gordon[1]

EVERY SUMMER UNTOLD NUMBERS of people descend on the beaches for their annual vacation ritual. My father did it with our family, and I (Philip) do it with my own now.

In fact, for Angie and me, our first family trip to the beach with both boys is like our family fish tale—it keeps growing! At this point it seems as if we carried all of our worldly possessions to the Gulf Coast. Each morning I would make multiple trips from our hotel room down what seemed fifty-six flights of stairs to set up our area on the beach. With blankets, bags, toys, floats, and a massive array of buckets, we were prepared for fun in the sun. After my half-dozen excursions were done, Angie and our boys would come down for an action-packed morning.

The only problem was that our sons were ages four and two. One would face plant in the sand and cry. The other would just jump up and down in front of the water, terrified of the waves. And, after about twenty-five minutes of "fun," everyone was tired, and we would go back to the room to recover.

But then something amazing happened. One afternoon both of the boys wanted to get in the water. If you've not been in the Gulf of Mexico, a great effect happens periodically. There are no curls to the waves. The water gets calm, and waves just look like speed bumps moving into shore. Suddenly they wanted to be in the water with mom and dad. So we put them on their floats and pushed them into the deep. Way to go, boys! You're on your own now!

I know what you're thinking. And of course we didn't do that. It's too dangerous. The water is too deep for toddlers. But the most dangerous part of the Gulf, the ocean, or any sea is the part that is not even visible—the undercurrent. When the Gulf of Mexico is calm, it is like a gentle friend that slowly carries you down the beach so you can see the sights. But, when the waves are stronger and the surf is up a bit, you quickly find yourself pulled out too far from the beach. On the beaches of the Atlantic or Pacific Oceans, the undercurrent can pull you out to sea or, even worse, drag you under and take your life.

However, my boys are no longer toddlers. They are teenagers. When we go to the beach, I rarely worry about them thrashing around in the surf. They float farther down the beach than some parents would allow. They often swim out farther than they should, and I'll call them back. But, generally, now when we're at the beach, it's up to them to stay close to us. A far cry from ten years ago when I constantly stayed close to them.

Now that they are older and more mature (in theory at least), they should be able to handle the undercurrent or undertow. To prepare them, I taught them a simple lesson: danger begins with an understated movement—drifting.

> *Danger begins with an understated movement—drifting.*

The Subtle Danger

The word *drifting* sounds so innocuous as if there is no danger at all. But the subtle beginning can lead to a long journey in the wrong direction. The same is true for believers. No one sets out to drift far from Christ, but many find themselves at a distance nonetheless. The story is usually one of losing perspective, less engagement with truth, and eventual change in our priorities. It is the loss of our first love described in the Bible. We have no intention to fail miserably in our discipleship journey.

So where does the failure occur? For our kids drifting down the coastline, failure did not occur when they were half a mile away. The failure occurred at the first moment when they lost attention to their surroundings and position. The fault is in the moment they ceased in their efforts to stay within the proper boundaries set by their parents. It was the subtle thought of, *Does it really matter that I stay this close?*

When it comes to our faith, the answer is a loud, bold, earth-shaking YES!

Drifting leads to a change in our heart. The less attention given to a person, the less affection will occur. The old adage, "Absence makes the heart grow fonder," is simply not true for our journey toward transformational discipleship. Absence, in fact, causes callousness. Billie Hanks told us in our interview with him about discipleship: "The essential definition of a disciple is one who has become a disciplined follower, a disciplined learner of our Lord."

> *Drifting brings about a tolerance for distance.*

Drifting and disobedience also go hand in hand. Getting out of view of their parents, children are more likely to play by their own rules. Think about a toddler who is left alone in a room with markers and no adult supervision. All of the previous "don't draw on the wall" instructions simply vanish from the child's mind. The same is true of a teenager once a driver's license is obtained or many kids who move to another city to attend college. Absence from the one who has authority will lead to a dismissal of the required way of life.

Drifting brings about a tolerance for distance. The first time we drift away, pretty immediately we catch where we went wrong and correct our actions. But if we keep allowing ourselves to drift, we go farther and farther each time. With thoughts like, *I've always made it back,* and, *I can still see where I need to get back to,* we tolerate the distance from God.

The Intentional Guard

God does not tolerate drifting by believers. The desire of the Spirit is to keep us close. Jesus spoke clearly in John 15:5–8 about the need to "remain" in Him.

> I am the vine; you are the branches. The one who
> remains in Me and I in him produces much fruit,
> because you can do nothing without Me. If anyone does
> not remain in Me, he is thrown aside like a branch and
> he withers. They gather them, throw them into the fire,

and they are burned. If you remain in Me and My words remain in you, ask whatever you want and it will be done for you. My Father is glorified by this: that you produce much fruit and prove to be My disciples.

Intentionality is needed to remain intimately related to Christ. We must intentionally humble ourselves since we are only the "branches" and He is the "vine." Later in this book the principles related to being in the right posture will be described more fully.

In the TD study believers acknowledge the need to seek after God as an attribute that should be present in their lives. When believers in the study were faced with the statement, "One of the main reasons I live my life the way I do is to please and honor God," most agreed, 78 percent (43 percent strongly and 35 percent somewhat). However, there is still room for improvement among believers. As leaders, we know that for a people to develop in their faith, they must prioritize God and His work in their lives.

The normal order of life for a disciple is to produce spiritual fruit. The fruit can come in the form of personal character and in the form of new believers. But, just as our salvation is the work of God we accept by faith, the fruit we can bear will come as we faithfully remain in Christ so God can work through us. A transformational disciple will produce more disciples from their personal ministry. They will also become and hopefully produce leaders for God's kingdom work in the world. We read in this passage that God's intention is that we will bear spiritual fruit. If He is so intentional about the results of our life, then we should be intentional about the manner of our life.

With the imagery of the vine and the branches, another lesson is one of our usefulness. The passage teaches that apart from Him we can do nothing. Separated from the vine, branches wither and lose their usefulness in producing fruit. The application is that when we no longer abide closely with Christ, we are incapable of producing more disciples for Him.

Transformational discipleship calls for a reshaping of how we view life, faith, and even Christ Himself. By engaging a lens of discipline, believers can see all of this better. More importantly, by using the discipline lens, believers can live more effectively for Christ.

Seeing Life Well

The purpose of a lens is to view things better. For some it means using contacts or eyeglasses to correct poor sight. For scientists, employing a microscope or telescope is for exploring that which cannot be seen with the naked eye. The lenses we use do not replace our eyes but enhance their abilities. Similarly, the discipline lens is to help us view life better. Specifically, it helps us understand God and how He is working in us.

The discipline lens is a way of viewing everything through the work of the gospel. It is prioritizing God's work, humbling ourselves before it, and making ourselves constantly available for it to be done through us.

The discipline lens is not intended just to offer a new set of rules. It is designed to help believers better engage with the truth of God's Word. After all, the worth of a lens is found in its ability to help the seer focus on that which is looked upon. For discipleship to be transformational, the disciple must look intently upon and into God's Word. Using the spiritual disciplines will aid in the journey toward Christian maturity.

Simply doing a group of random spiritual practices does not equate to spiritual maturity. Remember that all of us need to guard against information and legalism as the definitions of discipleship. By engaging the spiritual disciplines, information will be gained and boundaries to life practices will be drawn, but that is not the point. These are means to an end. But spiritual disciplines are never the end—Jesus is.

> **But spiritual disciplines are never the end— Jesus is.**

Giving Structure to Transformation

The spiritual disciplines are a set of practices used to draw us close to God. Believers should use disciplines to give a place for the Holy Spirit to speak and use God's Word in our lives. Whether you are in a public discipline of worshipping with the church or the private discipline of confessing your sin to Christ, these are structured activities the Spirit uses to move believers toward maturity.

Apart from grace-assisted effort, we are helpless to experience transformation. Looking at the Law in the Old Testament, we can easily feel overwhelmed. In the first five books of the Bible, we find an insurmountable number of laws. The laws God gave to His people ranged from how to worship in the temple to how to deal with skin diseases. They covered good business practices and what was allowable in a marriage. God looked at mankind's heart and knew we needed specific instructions to live a holy life. Everything was laid out in plain fashion. And, upon the construction of the temple, God placed His presence there for people to come and worship.

With the new covenant we have in Jesus Christ, the law has been fulfilled in the judicial sense. All of the laws we were not able to keep, Jesus kept. All of the laws we broke and punishment needed to be handed down, Jesus took the punishment deserved by the lawbreakers. And God's presence was no longer located in the holy of holies at the innermost room of the temple. With faith in Jesus, a Christian is given the deposit of the Holy Spirit.

> **The disciplines give a place of structure for transformational growth to occur.**

The role of the Spirit in our lives is particularly important to note when thinking about spiritual disciplines. As a person engages in study, fasting, service, or any of the disciplines, only by the Spirit's presence can transformation occur. Otherwise it is just religious machinations. The disciplines are activities that give time and space for the Spirit to give understanding about the truth presented in the Bible. When believers engage in spiritual activities, the Spirit can speak and move in our hearts. The disciplines give a place of structure for transformational growth to occur.

Loving Obedience

The Holy Spirit does something in our lives that cannot happen apart from Him. He is able to initiate the convergence between love and obedience. In John 14:15 Jesus said that if we love Him, then we will keep His commandments. In John 15 He reminded us that if we keep His commands, we will remain in His love. The two can only intersect when the Spirit is at work.

The Holy Spirit has the ability to align our desires with the will of God. One of the most common questions I (Eric) received as a pastor was, "How can I know the will of God?" The answer is both simple and complex: spend time with the Holy Spirit. In our life with the Spirit, we humble ourselves (get in the right posture) so He can teach us the plans for the kingdom. When we discipline ourselves to engage with Him relationally, then we will align with God's heart.

Most people ask about the will of God because they want to know what to do. The Spirit can alert us to the work of God around us. The issue that arises next is whether we will obey the directions He gives. At this point our love and our obedience must intersect if we are to forge ahead in His mission and our maturity.

Engaging the Disciplines

A delicate balance is needed when addressing specific spiritual disciplines. The temptation is to offer an easy five-step plan for spiritual success that should work for everyone. But there is not a one-size-fits-all plan for transformational discipleship. As we interviewed the experts from across the world, we discovered that different emphases work in different cultures. The same is true of churches in North America. For different congregations and for different believers, different methods are needed. In this section five generally accepted disciplines will be briefly described. We believe they are basic to the Christian life and foundational for growth. It is certainly not an exhaustive list but will help you begin leading disciples in the right direction.

Study

The first discipline to engage disciples with is Bible study. Paul wrote to the young pastor Timothy about the worth of the Scriptures. In 2 Timothy 3:16–17, he stated, "All Scripture is inspired by God and is profitable for teaching, for rebuking, for correcting, for training in righteousness, so that the man of God may be complete, equipped for every good work." The impact of the phrase "may be complete" has to do with maturity for life.

Through the Word, God is providing what is necessary for living as we should.

We are always puzzled by the neglect too many Christians give the Bible. Rarely do we engage in the rest of life without receiving some directions first. For example, many fathers have stayed up well into the night on Christmas Eve to assemble a bicycle, princess castle, or some other toy. We all know what the key is to making it as short a night as possible: the instructions. Of course, there are always those strong-headed parents who are convinced they can assemble the endless array of parts into the magical gift for the next morning. And they are the parents who awake bleary-eyed after a maddening night and only a few hours of sleep.

If we simply take a few minutes to read, understand, and decide to follow the instructions, everything goes more smoothly. The same is true in the believer's engagement with the Bible.

Reading, studying, and memorizing the Word are classic practices of the Christian life that bring us into alignment with God's will for us. We need to read in order to be familiar with the text. Believers should study so they understand the impact of the text. Disciples will memorize so they can fully apply the text. Engaging God's Word should be an all-consuming discipline for the believer.

Prayer

Any religion holding a belief in a higher power engages in prayer. For the other religions of the world, it is the practice to plead with the higher power to be generous or merciful or to strike down one's enemies. For the Christian, prayer is altogether different. Not only do we speak to God in prayer, but we also listen. Robert Coleman told our researchers, "The greatest opportunity will be when you're on your knees. The greatest ministry of discipling is prayer."

In the area of prayer, 76 percent of believers agree with the statement, "I find myself praying at the spur of the moment throughout the day." When asked about the amount of time that they set aside for prayer, 48 percent said they pray everyday, 25 percent a few times a week, and 8 percent once a week.

> *The greatest ministry of discipling is prayer.*

Regarding their private spiritual practices, believers were also asked how often they set aside time for private worship or thanksgiving. The study showed that 67 percent of believers do so at least once a week with 27 percent engaging in private worship daily. These are encouraging trends, but still we want to see believers push even further into how God is at work in their lives and in His mission.

Regarding prayer, Charles Spurgeon reportedly said, "Asking is the rule of the kingdom."[2] Earlier we looked at John 15; the seventh verse emphasizes this idea: "If you remain in Me and My words remain in you, ask whatever you want and it will be done for you." Putting it into the context of a believer who is relationally intimate with Christ and invested in His Word, then consequently making the proper petitions is a natural outcome. God expects that His people will make requests of Him for life's needs.

It is also the time in which God speaks to us. The Holy Spirit takes the time we give to prayer to teach us about the Scriptures. It is also the time He can align our will with His own. An image that can help here is that prayer is like a man adrift in a boat. Finding a rope and a hook, he throws it to the shore to secure it. As he pulls on the rope, is he pulling the shore to his boat or his boat to the shore? Obviously, the latter. Prayer works in the same fashion. It is a tool by which we align ourselves with what God is doing, not align God with what we are doing.

Silence

The natural inclination when thinking about something called a "discipline" is to consider it as an action to take. However, many of the disciplines are exercises in passivity. As will be emphasized repeatedly, for believers to get to the Transformational Sweet Spot, they must get into the proper posture. A portion of that posture necessitates quiet. Ecclesiastes 5:1–7 gives us some insight for this discipline.

> Guard your steps when you go to the house of God.
> Better to draw near in obedience than to offer the
> sacrifice as fools do, for they ignorantly do wrong. Do
> not be hasty to speak, and do not be impulsive to make
> a speech before God. God is in heaven and you are on
> earth, so let your words be few. For dreams result from
> much work and a fool's voice from many words. When
> you make a vow to God, don't delay fulfilling it, because
> He does not delight in fools. Fulfill what you vow. Better
> that you do not vow than that you vow and not fulfill
> it. Do not let your mouth bring guilt on you, and do
> not say in the presence of the messenger that it was a
> mistake. Why should God be angry with your words and
> destroy the work of your hands? For many dreams bring
> futility, so do many words. Therefore, fear God.

Solomon wrote the book of Ecclesiastes as a commentary on the desires of life. In what appears to be an odd interlude to the book, he reminds God's people of the need to be quiet before God. The passage communicates two sets of warnings. First, he tells believers to be careful in anything they vow or promise God. It is better to hold your tongue than to promise something you'll never follow through on.

Simply being quiet in God's presence is the second warning given. Solomon says to "guard your steps," "do not be hasty to speak and do not be impulsive to make a speech before God," and "let your words be few." Unfortunately most prayer lives are an ocean of talking with only a periodic interlude of silence. By human nature, hastiness is the default mode for most of us. We talk out of turn, share our opinions too quickly, and speak before we think. To position ourselves properly before God's truth, quiet is required. If we will be quiet for a few moments, God will speak and move and lead us.

Service

Spiritual growth is often considered to be the personal or private work of the believer. However, much of what we do in the Christian life is out in front of others. It is especially true when we engage in God's mission. Serving people—especially those who have nothing to give in return—requires growth on our part.

Service is not our natural inclination. Self-preservation is. Going public with your faith tests your commitment. As a discipline, service gives room for us to develop in our character. With the mission of God as our focus, transformation of our heart occurs as we experience God's work in our development. Service develops our love and refines our view of God's work.

As a discipline, service gives room for us to develop in our character.

As we prioritize the type of work God requires, the Macedonian call given to Paul in Acts 16:9 was, "Cross over to Macedonia and help us." When Paul arrived in Macedonia, he gave them the gospel. Certainly social needs were present in Macedonia. We know from the biblical and historical records that injustice was common. Poverty was rampant. Political oppression was a normal occurrence. Widows and orphans were powerless and needed an advocate. But Paul did not address those needs. Instead, his service to the Macedonians was to give them the gospel first. The truth was the lens through which he saw all of life. In his service to the lost and his ministry to the saved, the gospel was always prioritized.

Worship

A final spiritual discipline to highlight is worship. Now, again, we know that spiritual disciplines are normally thought of as private practices in our lives. Meanwhile, worship is normally considered to be a public activity. In worship God's people engage in speaking to God about what is most important—namely, God.

Remember, though, that the discipline lens helps us focus better on the truth. And the truth is found in the person of God. What God does and what He has said is the truth because it comes from Him. As believers focus their attention on Him, they will experience the transformation that comes from being in contact with the Lord. Don Whitney said: "We're to worship God privately. We're to worship with the church. We're to get into the Word of God privately. We're to get into the Word with the church."

But what exactly is worship? Perhaps it will help to be reminded of what it is not. Worship is not a music style. Nor is worship defined as a particular time slot. Worship is the activity by a believer or group of believers to celebrate God's goodness and work. As a discipline, worship occurs when we prioritize God in our thinking and in our affections for a particular period of time. In these moments we are encountering truth and being changed by it.

In the environment of worship, numbers of people have been transformed by the power of the gospel. Throughout the book of Acts, the disciples often had life-changing experiences during times of worship. During prayer and worship new apostles were appointed, missionaries were sent out by the Spirit, and people were confronted with their sins. In our day the experience is similar. During worship services when the truth is proclaimed, people come to understand the gospel and enter into Christ's salvation. For disciples our sin is confessed, our courage is renewed, and our mission is better understood. It is a transformational experience.

More disciplines could be listed and explored, but these five are a good place for any church to begin. As you engage in the practice of these or any disciplines, continue to place your attention on truth first and the activity second. God is more concerned that you encounter Him than He is that you complete a religious activity well.

Becoming Something Else

In theological language discipleship is about our sanctification. It transforms us so that we may be like Christ. The point of the disciplines is to move us toward this godliness. They are tools in the hands of our Savior to do something extraordinary through ordinary practices.

The members of our churches know about many of the basic disciplines that will lead them to a posture where transformation can take place. From the TD research, we found that believers recognize that spiritual practices are important. Setting aside time for prayer, confession of sin, and

> *The point of the disciplines is to move us toward this godliness.*

praying for the lost was seen as important. Additionally, reading the Bible regularly as a discipline is one of the most likely indicators for spiritual growth. And being discipled by others was also recorded as a valuable practice for discipleship to occur.

We are not convinced that discipleship is happening at a deep enough level in the lives of Christians in North America. Hopefully, though, these statistics show that believers are moving in the right direction toward transformation.

Martin Luther was a monk who could not find peace with the ritual, legalism, and regulations in the Roman Catholic Church. Eventually, upon closer study of the idea of salvation by grace through faith, he dissented against the church. This solitary monk began the Protestant Reformation. He wrote the following about the process of sanctification.

> This life therefore is not righteousness but growth in
>   righteousness;
> not health but healing;
> not being but becoming;
> not rest but exercise.
> We are not yet what we shall be, but we are growing
>   toward it.
> The process is not finished, but it is going on.
> This is not the end, but it is the road.
> All does not yet gleam in glory, but all is being purified.[3]

The discipline lens leads believers toward transformation by keeping the focus off of the disciplines and placing it on the truth of the gospel. Remember, the natural state of our hearts is to drift. But by exercising grace-infused disciplines, we can keep our eyes upon Christ's work in us. Building on what Luther wrote, we can look beyond the temporary and see the eternal.

Part 2

Transformational Framework: POSTURE

The Transformational Sweet Spot
is the intersection of truth given by healthy leaders
to someone in a vulnerable posture.

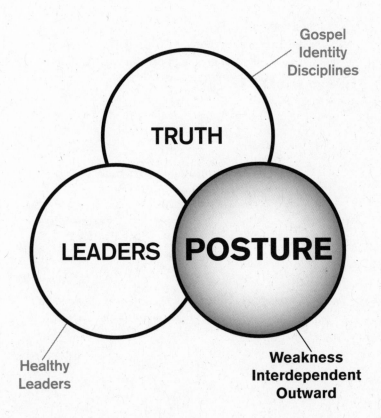

*He leads the humble in what is right
and teaches them His way.*

(Ps. 25:9)

• • •

*For Yahweh takes pleasure in His people; He adorns
the humble with salvation.*

(Ps. 149:4)

• • •

*But He said to me, "My grace is sufficient for you, for
power is perfected in weakness." Therefore, I will most
gladly boast all the more about my weaknesses, so that
Christ's power may reside in me.*

(2 Cor. 12:9)

• • •

*God resists the proud, but gives grace to
the humble. . . . Draw near to God and
He will draw near to you.*

(James 4:6, 8)

• • •

*Humble yourselves, therefore, under the mighty
hand of God, so that He may exalt at the proper time.*

(1 Pet. 5:6)

POSTURE

If you're really as tough as your defenses, let them fall.
—Jimmy Eat World

BEFORE OUR HOLY AND powerful God, everyone is vulnerable and weak. His weakness is stronger than our strength, and His foolishness is wiser than our wisdom (1 Cor. 1:25). All who seek to come before Him are humbled by His greatness.

We often attempt to cover our weakness with status, achievement, money, or relationships. All of these crumble before Him, and our reliance on these things only further reveals our weakness.

When we attempt to stand strong in our own merit or goodness trusting the lesser gods and the fragile coverings of our weakness, God only knows us from a distance (Ps. 138:6). But when we humbly acknowledge our weakness, God steps in with His transforming power.

God is attracted to weakness.

God works in our weakness, pain, and vulnerability. Transformation often occurs when the truth of God is applied to a person in a humble posture. Again, we are hoping not to present the transformational framework as a magical formula. At the same time we see the premise of a vulnerable posture in both Scripture and the research.

As a leader passionate about God transforming others, you have likely experienced the following scenario:

You present the truth of God to a group of people, and the response is radically different. As you are teaching, discussing, counseling, shepherding, or leading, you know in your spirit that one person is really grabbing hold of the truth. His heart is melted. God is clearly at work, and fruit begins to show in his life.

At the same time, someone else in your circle of influence is being confronted with the same truth. With the same passion and prayerfulness, you humbly seek to apply the timeless truth of God to his heart. But there is no change, and you know it deep down in your gut. The truth lands on a hard or prideful heart.

Same truth, yet a different response; the difference is the posture.

While God changes people through His truth, people are most likely to receive the transformative truth of God when they are in a vulnerable posture. Over the next three chapters we will share three postures of vulnerability as we continue to move toward our understanding of the Transformational Sweet Spot. We will discover that transformation often occurs when disciples are in a posture of weakness, interdependence, and/or with an outward focus.

As a church or ministry leader, prayerfully consider how you may help people live in a vulnerable position before God and how you may redeem seasons of vulnerability for transformation.

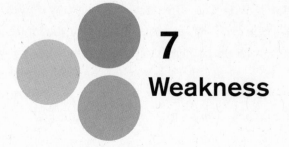

7
Weakness

Storms produce growth.

—John Owen

THE MOST OVERWHELMING INTERVIEWS with believers concerning seasons of intense spiritual growth affirms that God uses
trials, pain, and suffering to lovingly put His own into a posture of
weakness resulting in deep transformation. Of course the interviews only give illustrative material to what the Scriptures clearly
teach; God graciously uses suffering, opposition, and overwhelming circumstances to perfect His own.

Historically we have read of extraordinary cases of pastors in
the Middle East imprisoned for their faith, missionaries oppressed
for their gospel work, or families becoming outcasts for convert-
ing to Christ. In such circumstances, when giving up one's faith is
the natural inclination of the human heart, they chose humbly to
submit to God in the midst of unbelievable trials.

In our day we have personally watched as people grew in their faith during times of suffering. In fact, many believers will later speak of the blessing of the trial and how because of it they matured even more in their faith. One such example is my (Philip) friend Bob. Every Sunday I watch him hobble into the church building with his cane in one hand and towing his rolling briefcase in the other. Bob serves as an elder at our church and knows more about prayer than many could imagine. Over the last year Bob has endured excruciating pain as his hip joints deteriorated and were replaced.

Having been a believer for some time, he could have shook a fist at God and asked the all-too-common question, "Why me?" but he has not. Instead, lying on his back in hospital rooms, rehab centers, and at home, Bob prayed for God to strengthen him. And God answered. Now, with the solitude gained in the seclusion of those beds, he has been strengthened in his faith rather than been defeated by the temporary circumstances of life's difficulties.

> Leonard Sweet said, "Strengths are all about possibilities. Weaknesses are about impossibilities."

As you look at the lives of those people you consider to know something about following Jesus—those who continue to experience true transformation and walk in an ever-deepening way with God—there is almost always something that unites them. It's not their race, their age, their socioeconomic background, or their occupation. More times than not, these people have been marked at one time or another by a period of great struggle. In them we see the hand of God at work not only sustaining them through seasons of hardship and pain but actually taking them to places of spiritual intimacy they never would have gone without suffering.

The road to some places of spiritual depth is often paved with tears. As Leonard Sweet said, "Strengths are all about possibilities. Weaknesses are about impossibilities."

Suffering

Holocaust survivor Victor Frankl said, "Despair is suffering without meaning."[1] For the believer even what initially feels like meaningless suffering always has meaning because God lovingly uses suffering to transform His own.

Exercising faith is an attribute of transformational discipleship necessary to grow in spite of suffering. When believers were asked to deal with the statement, "During difficult circumstances, I sometimes doubt that God loves me and will provide for my life," its received an overwhelming disagreement by the believers. In all, 78 percent disagreed with the statement (56 percent strongly). When disciples are being transformed by Christ, they show a confidence that God is active in providing for their needs in every circumstance.

Apostles James and Peter on different occasions reminded believers that their suffering would result in maturity. Both apostles wrote to believers persecuted and scattered around the world:

> Consider it a great joy, my brothers, whenever you
> experience various trials, knowing that the testing of
> your faith produces endurance. But endurance must
> do its complete work, so that you may be mature and
> complete, lacking nothing. (James 1:2–4)

> You rejoice in this, though now for a short time you have
> had to struggle in various trials so that the genuineness
> of your faith—more valuable than gold, which perishes

though refined by fire—may result in praise, glory, and
honor at the revelation of Jesus Christ. (1 Pet. 1:6–7)

Like us, the apostle Paul begged for his suffering to be taken
from him, but he learned that God's grace is enough in the midst of
them. He learned that when we are weak, God makes us strong in
Him (2 Cor. 12:10). Paul taught that part of the maturing process
includes suffering just as Christ suffered (Phil. 3:10) and that
suffering is actually promised to the believer (Phil. 1:29).

Messages that hint to listeners that suffering decreases in this
life are lies; they contradict the clear teaching of Scripture that
God has chosen to use suffering lovingly to transform the hearts
of His people. Job was the God-fearing and blameless man that
God pointed to as an example of faithfulness, and God allowed
intense suffering into Job's life. Allowed by God to touch his life,
Satan took away Job's business, wealth, health, and children. Yet
Job still worshipped God. He did so even when his wife counseled
him to curse God and die.

The bulk of the book of Job is the discussion between Job and
his three friends who came to him with insight and advice about
suffering. They offered answers church people still sometimes offer
today: "God must be disciplining you," and, "There must be some
sin in your life." Their ridiculous attempts to explain Job's suffering
were met with God's ire.

Job's life was utterly ruined; he lost everything. His friends
could barely recognize him, as his appearance was appalling from
sores. Job begged God for the reason as he longed to understand
why all the pain occurred.

God never came to Job with the answer, but He did come with
Himself.[2]

The interaction between God and Job is one of the most intense chapters in the Bible (Job 38). Job was given a greater understanding of God through the painful posture of suffering. And he was a more humble man before the sovereignty and comfort of God. In the end God restored all things to Job (Job 42:10).

While Job's restoration is exciting to read, it is merely a foretaste of the ultimate restoration that occurs in eternity for believers. Though the latter half of Job's life was twice as full as the first half of his life, eternity is infinitely richer and greater than anything we experience in this life.

About future restoration for believers, the apostle Paul wrote, "For I consider that the sufferings of this present time are not worth comparing with the glory that is going to be revealed to us" (Rom. 8:18). Paul suffered intensely and never diminished the experience of the pain in our present life. He was reminding believers that the intensity of present pain only points to the immensity of future glory.

The phrase "not worth comparing" paints the picture of scales where suffering is measured against the future glory. The suffering is real, but times of suffering are light and momentary compared to the weight and significance of the restoration promised believers (2 Cor. 4:17). Our future glory weighs more in terms of intensity and duration.

> **Suffering has a way of causing believers to remember what really matters.**

Eternal pleasure is infinitely more enjoyable than the current suffering is painful, and the joys of eternity never end.[3]

Suffering has a way of causing believers to remember what really matters. As painful as suffering is, trials are treasures because they separate triviality from reality.[4] They awaken us and foster greater dependence on the Lord.

Opposition

No one enjoys being disliked, misunderstood, misrepresented, misquoted, hated, or persecuted. Yet God assures His followers that persecution will come and that He will use it for transforming His disciples (Phil. 1:29; 2 Tim. 3:12).

The Old Testament tells the story of King David. As a young man David faced intense opposition from King Saul for many years, and the opposition caused David humbly and passionately to seek God. Ironically, when David lived as a fugitive in a cave, he pursued God with great intensity; and when he lived as king in a palace, he pursued a married woman that was not his own.

King Saul asked David to lead his own army and marry his own daughter. But the only reason for doing so was to keep a close eye on David. Saul's intense jealousy of David caused him to try personally to take David's life on two occasions—both times by hurtling spears at him. So David became a fugitive from the king he loved and in the country he would one day rightfully rule.

David fled to Ramah to see the prophet Samuel and then headed to Nob to meet with a priest. There he took possession of the sword Israel took off of Goliath after David killed him. Now the once-heralded hero is a man on the run. Gathering a small army of four hundred soldiers, David finds himself hiding in caves to survive the wrath of the king. Many biblical scholars believe David fled for almost an entire decade.

An entire decade of his life seemingly ruined by one egomaniac. From a cave in the area known as En-gedi, David penned these words:

Be gracious to me, God, be gracious to me, for I take
refuge in You. I will seek refuge in the shadow of Your
wings until danger passes. I call to God Most High, to
God who fulfills His purpose for me. He reaches down
from heaven and saves me, challenging the one who
tramples me. Selah God sends His faithful love and
truth. I am surrounded by lions; I lie down with those
who devour men. Their teeth are spears and arrows;
their tongues are sharp swords. God, be exalted above
the heavens; let Your glory be over the whole earth. They
prepared a net for my steps; I was despondent. They dug
a pit ahead of me, but they fell into it! Selah. My heart is
confident, God, my heart is confident. I will sing; I will
sing praises. Wake up, my soul! Wake up, harp and lyre!
I will wake up the dawn. I will praise You, Lord, among
the peoples; I will sing praises to You among the nations.
For Your faithful love is as high as the heavens; Your
faithfulness reaches the clouds. God, be exalted above the
heavens; let Your glory be over the whole earth. (Ps. 57)

He is satisfied in the cave, not in the comfort of a palace. He
is filled with joy while facing opposition, not while enjoying songs
written about his feats on the battlefield. In the middle of painful opposition, David learned that God's love and faithfulness are
enough. Twice he mentions God's love in the psalm because his
heart has been melted by God's unconditional acceptance of him.

Through the pain David found his approval and his acceptance
in God; therefore, he was already approved and accepted and did
not need or crave others' approval. Saul lived for others' approval,
and he was miserable in a palace. David found his approval in God,
and he woke up the dawn with his singing while hiding in a cave.

The pain put David in a posture to run to God. The cave was not David's refuge; God was. Transformation occurs when someone runs to God in the midst of pain, not to the bottle, relationships, more work, pornography, or other shaky caves. David confessed his absolute dependence on God, needing to rest completely in God's wings as a baby chicken rests in the wings of a parent. Instead of attempting to "bow up" or "stand strong," David remained weak and fragile before God, and God filled him with great joy and strength. David trusted that God would use the opposition to fulfill God's ultimate purpose for David (v. 2). David knew that God was developing his character through the pain, preparing him for something greater.

> **The cave was not David's refuge; God was.**

In the midst of opposition from others, David grew in his understanding of his approval before God; and because his heart was refreshed with God's acceptance and kindness, he was able to express forgiveness even to those who hated him most.

According to 1 Samuel 24 Saul enters the same cave David is in to use the bathroom. He disrobes, puts himself in a sitting position, and faces outward. David has the prime opportunity to come behind him and kill him. David's men are encouraging David to kill Saul in epic fashion. When you read the story, perhaps you yell at the pages as well.

"He has chased you for years, spread countless lies about you to justify his pursuit, and has ruined your life. You can kill him in this humiliating position and make everything right. Go for it David!"

David does not kill Saul but expresses love and forgiveness to him. He is able to love and forgive because he is first overwhelmed with God as his refuge, as the place of ultimate security.

When the people you serve face opposition, it is an invitation for transformation to have the heart reminded that ultimate acceptance and approval come not from others but from God. Seeing the story through the lens of the gospel reminds us that our hearts are only transformed when we are in awe of another King who lived in the same region. The King of kings, the completely pure and innocent One, was persecuted and faced intense opposition—much more so than David. As David spared Saul, God spared us and accepted us as we are; therefore, we no longer need to live for the acceptance of others.

Overwhelming Circumstances

Many broken clichés have failed to give accurate perspective on weakness. Some church and ministry leaders have preached, "God will not give you more than you can handle." Actually He will give you way more than you can handle in your own strength. In His goodness He will allow life to overwhelm you so that you will humbly need His strength and wisdom.

Believers know this to be true. The TD research posed the following statement to Christians: "I believe that God has a purpose for all events in my life, regardless of whether I perceive each event as being good or bad." Incredibly, 71 percent strongly agreed, and 21 percent agreed somewhat. The overwhelming majority—92 percent—of believers agree that God is purposeful in what He allows us to encounter.

Leaders have also articulated that "God helps those who help themselves," which has motivated many people to work hard and expect God to "fill in the spaces." The reality of the gospel is that God helps the helpless. When we realize that we are utterly helpless without His grace and power in our lives, we are in a vulnerable posture that welcomes His transformation.

Unfortunately we are masters of self-protection. Entire industries in the first world have been built around removing uncertainty and vulnerability from life. We have insurance for everything and then supplementary insurance in case the first set isn't enough. We try to prepare for every contingency so that we never have a moment when we are out of control.

> *The reality of the gospel is that God helps the helpless.*

While many of these things are good when viewed in their proper context, they are at best, an illusion. We do not have control of our own lives, much less anyone else's. It only takes the slightest shakeup into the well-worn plans for our lives to remind us of that.

When someone becomes a parent for the first time, there is maybe a day or two of bliss when all the baby is, is "cute." He or she is delivered to the room of the parents first thing in the morning and then taken away at night. You sleep well in that hospital bed, dining on the green Jell-o of luxury. But then comes going-home day. A well-mannered nurse wheels the new mom to the curb of the hospital with their bundle of joy and then . . . leaves her there— no instruction book. It's an overwhelming circumstance indeed to realize that you have been entrusted with a life to completely care for and shape.

Then there is the moment when "love" stops being an emotion and starts being a choice. When you are first married, you can't imagine a time when you don't want to spend every waking minute with each other, when every day is better than the last. But then the strangest thing starts to happen—you get on each other's nerves. The way she slurps her soup. The way he hangs the toilet paper.

And suddenly you realize that marriage is work. It's hard work. And you even begin to have that creeping, nagging thought: *What have I gotten myself into?*

Or perhaps the time when you start a new job that everyone in the world thinks you'll do great at, but you know the truth: This role is beyond you. It's bigger than your intelligence, your leadership ability, and your creativity. There are far too many aspects to keep track of, and you know it's only a matter of time until you are exposed as the fraud you know you are.

These are overwhelming circumstances, and in them we have one of two choices. First, we can try to escape. Most of us go that route, and we escape through all sorts of means. Some of those means are more innocuous than others—we escape into our work schedule, into entertainment, or even into church—anywhere we can find a sense of that lost control. But other times our desire to escape leads us into quicker ruin. We run into the arms of someone other than our spouse. To a drug of choice. Or, if you were someone like Gideon, you might escape into a winepress.

The book of Judges is a depressingly cyclical book. The people of Israel lapse into sin and idolatry, and God brings about their oppression. When things get too bad, they call out to God, and He responds by raising up a deliverer—a judge who is endowed with the Spirit of God in order to do mighty feats and restore God's people. When we meet Gideon, one of these would-be deliverers of the nation of Israel, he looks like anything but. He's hiding—escaping—from an overwhelming set of circumstances.

The oppression in those days was coming from the Midianites, a part of a nomadic confederation of peoples who were much like the grasshoppers in the Pixar film, *A Bug's Life*. The poor (yet idolatrous) Israelites would work hard all year to plant their crops; and just when the freshly seeded crops were sprouting, the Midianites would cross the Jordan to pillage and destroy. After seven years of this, the nation was devastated:

> Whenever the Israelites planted crops, the Midianites, Amalekites, and the Qedemites came and attacked them. They encamped against them and destroyed the produce of the land, even as far as Gaza. They left nothing for Israel to eat, as well as no sheep, ox or donkey. For the Midianites came with their cattle and their tents like a great swarm of locusts. They and their camels were without number, and they entered the land to waste it. So Israel became poverty-stricken because of Midian, and the Israelites cried out to the LORD. (Judg. 6:3–6)

Literally, verse 6 tells us that the Israelites "became small" because of Midian. They were belittled in every way, shape, and form as these circumstances pressed down on them. And that sense of smallness in the face of their circumstances was the reason Gideon was cowering outside of view.

Specifically, Gideon was in a wine vat, but he wasn't making wine. He was threshing wheat. That's a process of beating the cut stalks, discarding the straw, and then tossing the remaining mixture up into the air. The heavier grain would fall to the ground, but the chaff would just blow away. Problem is, during Gideon's day, the Midianites were like locusts, and the sight of grain being thrown up in the air would undoubtedly attract attention. So Gideon was hiding, in a smallish kind of way, pressed by his circumstances into trying in secret to eek out survival.

But into these overwhelming circumstances steps the Angel of the Lord. While Gideon was wringing his hands in worry and frustration, the angel leisurely watches (perhaps with a smirk on his face): "The Angel of the LORD came, and He sat under the oak that was in Ophrah, which belonged to Joash, the Abiezrite. His son Gideon was threshing wheat in the wine vat in order to hide it from the Midianites" (Judg. 6:11).

Do you see the beautiful contrast? The man is overwhelmed; God is in control. The man is cowering; God is relaxing. The man is working feverishly in the shadows; God is sitting under the shade of an oak tree. Such is the case with all the circumstances that make us feel small. We may rest assured that not one of them has knocked God off His throne or caused a bead of sweat to appear on His brow.

From our TD research, it is encouraging to find that believers have a different view from Gideon and his fellow Israelites. Rather than hiding, they express the intention to live anywhere God directs, work any job that God hands to

> **The man is cowering; God is relaxing.**

them, or help anyone they find in need. It indicates that a believer will likely grow when they exercise their faith by setting aside time for private worship or thanksgiving to God—certainly a far cry from Gideon's hiding strategy. Faith is exercised when believers engage in Bible study groups that cost them time and effort. In the midst of understanding our weakness, the grace-oriented activities of searching for God's heart and caring for God's mission lead believers toward transformational growth.

Even when the unexpected arises that interrupts the normal comforts of life, the transformed disciple is ready to follow God into His will. Even when seemingly insurmountable circumstances mount against us, we have the opportunity in our weakness to rejoice in a God who is strong enough to rest under the oak tree.

Weakness through the Gospel Lens

The necessary embrace of weakness is one of the defining characteristics of Christianity. As an insult in the Roman Empire, it was said that Christianity was the religion of women and slaves. True enough. The reason, in that culture, so many of those who were overlooked by societal standards flocked to the gospel was because of the intrinsic weakness associated with it.

Believing the gospel requires weakness on the part of the believer. Think about the core message of the gospel regarding the condition of people—it's one of absolute powerlessness. Helplessness. Desperately great need. It's no wonder Paul described the common state of humanity apart from Christ in such negative terms:

> And you were dead in your trespasses and sins in
> which you previously walked according to this world,
> according to the ruler who exercises authority over the
> lower heavens, the spirit now working in the disobedient.
> We too all previously lived among them in our fleshly
> desires, carrying out the inclinations of our flesh and
> thoughts, and we were by nature children under wrath.
> (Eph. 2:1–3)

Notice the specific word choice here. According to Paul, we don't need a little help. We're not "almost good enough." The cross doesn't simply push us over the edge in God's good graces. The picture here isn't of someone who is struggling but of someone who is dead. The dead don't need help; they need a miracle.

We should remember this simple lesson: We don't have a sin problem. We have a death problem.

The dead are in an absolute state of weakness, unable to alter their condition. Instead, their condition must be altered from an outside force. This is the entrance to the gospel. It is for people of minimal reputation, means, and power that have the shortest distance to fall to get to the rock-bottom place of understanding the depth of their need.

But after humbling ourselves to enter the kingdom, something strange happens. Pride lurks around every corner, and soon we find ourselves leaving that place of weakness. We begin slowly and subtly to trust in our ability to obey God and deny sin. Weakness is replaced by supposed strength. Somehow this trust in our own ability is what passes for discipleship in many people's lives.

To put it another way, we have the tendency to think that our justification is accomplished by Jesus but our growth is accomplished by us. We treat the gospel as if it were the starting blocks of the race of life. We brace ourselves against it and push off, but then we're on our own. The speed at which we run is based on our own muscles. We become Christian legalists.

Transformational discipleship, from a biblical standpoint, is different. Rather than an initial posture of weakness, real discipleship involves a perpetual recognition of our great need. Because of this, the gospel isn't the starting blocks of the race; the gospel is the track itself. It's the basis for the way we run every day of our lives.

We found that believers growing in their faith consistently disagreed with the ideas that change was not possible in their lives or transformation possible in the lives of non-Christians. They believe that when we trust Christ, growth occurs. There is a sense among TD believers that God accomplishes the inexplicable when we submit to His work in us.

Paul reminded the Corinthians believers of this in 1 Corinthians 15:1–2 when he wrote, "Now brothers, I want to clarify for you the gospel I proclaimed to you; you received it and have taken your stand on it. You are also saved by it." The church then and we today need to be reminded that only the gospel can do this work. It's the means by which they were saved, in which they are standing, and by which they will continue into glory. When we remind ourselves of the gospel every day, we will recognize the truth that we need the cross as much today as we did yesterday. And tomorrow we will need it again.

Weakness through the Identity Lens

As we've established, an essential part of transformational discipleship is understanding our new identity in Christ. From that new identity behavior rightly flows. Weakness through the identity lens, then, is often the means God uses to remind us of who we really are. We desperately need reminding.

When all is well in life, the bank accounts are full, and everyone has a clean bill of health, we have a tendency to drift toward marks of self-identification apart from Christ. We might define ourselves by the behavior of our children, by our aptitude for running marathons, or by the number of people who comment on our witty tweets. Slowly but methodically, we find our self-worth and definition in these things. We become so sure of who we are that we fail to live with a sense of weakness and desperation, clinging to what God says about us. The apostle Peter is a textbook example in this case.

Here was one confident in his own strength. He was on the mount of transfiguration. He was the one who boldly confessed that Jesus was the Christ. He was the one willing to swing his legs out of the boat and walk on water toward the Son of God (at least for a little while). Peter was so confident of himself that when Jesus told the disciples they would all desert Him, Peter felt the need to defend Himself: "Even if everyone runs away, I will certainly not!" (Mark 14:29).

That's a far different cry from the Peter we find in John 21. In this passage, after Peter's outright denial of Jesus during His crucifixion and the subsequent resurrection, Peter has gone back to where he felt most comfortable: the sea. He was fishing, because what else could he do? He had done the unthinkable. He had betrayed and denied His friend, His master, despite his bravado. Peter had shown the true weakness inside him when he was pressed, and he wasn't hanging onto much hope. He once fancied himself a great leader, a man of courage and conviction, but now he knew the truth: he was just a fisherman. He was foolish to think any different.

But then comes the wonderful scene of restoration. Jesus makes breakfast for His friend and asks him one question three times: "Do you love Me?" The word Jesus chose for love is intentional. He asked Peter if he loved Him with an *agape*, a Christlike, love. But gone was the man who was willing to time and time again step up to the plate.

Each time Peter responded that he did love Jesus but not the way Jesus was asking. Peter said he loved Jesus with a *phileo* kind of love, the love one friend has for another. This is Peter's recognition of the sad truth of himself—that despite his best efforts he had failed and that he was likely to fail again. No more empty promises.

Notice, though, how Jesus responded. He doesn't berate Peter. He doesn't bring up his failure. Instead He commissions him:

"Do you love me?"

"Feed My sheep," Jesus said. "I assure you: When you were young, you would tie your belt and walk wherever you wanted. But when you grow old, you will stretch out your hands and someone else will tie you and carry you where you don't want to go." He said this to signify by what kind of death he would glorify God. After saying this, He told him, "Follow Me!" (John 21:17–19)

Jesus reminded Peter, in this moment of great honesty and transparency, that all was not lost. Sure, Peter had lost his courage and reputation, the marks he thought made him who he was. But Jesus reminded him of who he really was. Though Peter couldn't see it at the moment, Jesus told him about the core of who he was.

Opposition, overwhelming circumstances, and suffering remove from us all the things we might be tempted to count on. We find ourselves stripped of those things that we think make us who we are. But in these moments, when we feel so naked, Jesus is willing to step in and remind us that no matter what else happens, we are His followers. We are His disciples . . . and His brothers and sisters.

Discipline Lens

Spiritual disciplines can only be rightly accomplished through a realization of weakness. Without that all these practices will only lead us to pride and an effort to merit the favor of God through our works. We will begin to read the Bible, pray, fast, and do all other spiritual disciplines because we think God will like us better.

This is a radical corruption of these tools for godliness given to us for transformational discipleship. But when accomplished from a spirit of great dependency and recognition of weakness, these tools of grace can move us further into the life of discipleship God has for us.

But how do we do that? It's a particularly difficult question since we are now talking in the realm of the attitude of the heart. That is to say, the same act done by two different people might seemingly be no different from the perspective of an outside observer. And yet one of those actions might serve to glorify God and uplift the Christian while the same act might move another person down the road to ruin. In order to practice the disciplines, then, with the perspective of weakness, we must continually remind ourselves of exactly what the right purpose of those disciplines is.

We do not pray, fast, or memorize the Bible to earn God's favor. Nor do we do these things in order to merit God's blessings, to barter with Him for healing or money or anything else. We practice these disciplines in order to position ourselves rightly to keep in step with the Spirit. An illustration might help here.

> *We practice these disciplines in order to position ourselves rightly to keep in step with the Spirit.*

Think about it in terms of boats. If you picture yourself on a rowboat, the spiritual disciplines are like the oars. You put the oars in the water, but the distance you travel is proportional to the strength of your own shoulders. So the extent to which you follow Jesus and know Him better is equivalent to the tenacity with which you, in your own will and strength, read the Bible, pray, and everything else.

If you picture yourself in a speedboat, then there's not much use for oars at all. All you do is turn the key and let the motor take over. You're just along for the ride. In this scenario, you don't really need the disciplines at all. They're nice to have and good practices to be sure, but in the end you're really just "letting go and letting

God." He's going to move and position you where He wants you to be anyway, right? Just hold on for heaven.

But think about the disciplines now in terms of a sailboat. There is much work to do on this kind of vessel. There are knots to be tied and sails to be raised. This is hard labor, but in the end all you are really doing is positioning your craft for the wind. And you can't control the wind. You are, then, still in a position of weakness despite your best efforts. This is the right way to practice the disciplines with an ingrained sense of weakness. Reading the Bible, prayer, fasting, and all the rest are the means by which you position your life to receive the life-giving breath and strength of the Spirit on a day-to-day basis. Every time you practice these disciplines, you are putting yourself in that position—a position that is radically dependent on the Spirit of God, which, ironically, is in fact directly translated from Greek to be "divine wind."

Implications for Ministry Leaders

The reality of a "weak posture" being essential for maturation is challenging for ministry leaders because we obviously won't program for these moments. While ministry leaders must design environments that promote a posture of interdependence or outward focus, it would be ministry malpractice for fallible and finite leaders to plan painful events for people. Leaders should never hope for the accident, divorce, miscarriage, cancer, unemployment, or overwhelming circumstance. But as leaders we must understand that God's grace in those moments is often experienced in transformational ways.

In the midst of pain, ministry leaders must resist the temptation to offer trite clichés or apply Bible verses haphazardly. While Romans 8:28 is true and perfect, the verse must be applied to the heart carefully and with great timing. Instead of offering words as Job's three friends did, leaders should simply be there. Words are not remembered, but presence is.[5]

So what should ministry leaders do in the midst of pain to maximize those moments for transformation.

Prepare people for the pain.

Prepare people for pain by teaching the truth of living in a fallen world ravaged with the effects of sin, the hope of the future when everything is made right, and the reality that God lovingly uses pain to purify and mature His people. Remind people that God is ultimately in control of everything, that He does whatever He pleases, and that this life is brief and temporary. Grab the hearts of the people you serve with the great news of heaven where every sorrow will be reversed and all the implications of a fallen world will be gone forever.

Prepare the ministry culture for pain.

Since people are most likely to be transformed when placed in a vulnerable posture, often by weakness, then there are major implications for church leaders to ensure people are shepherded well through these seasons.

People are often most open to visiting a church or ministry when going through a difficult trial (divorce, death, sickness, etc.), feeling deeply overwhelmed (new job, relocation, new child, etc.), or experiencing emotional pain (sudden empty nesters, foreclosure, job loss, etc.). As these people walk into a church in those moments, how they are treated matters greatly. Imagine someone coming to your church this weekend internally crushed with pain. How will your church respond to him? Is your church prepared to greet and honor people with biblical hospitality?

In those painful moments people are often looking for others in similar situations, others who can empathize and walk with them through the pain. Is your church or ministry prepared to help those in pain develop relationships with others?

In moments of recognized weakness, people are often looking for direction, wisdom, or counsel. They will search for someone to listen, someone to offer insight into their pain. Is your church prepared to counsel people through the pain?

We are not advocating a particular strategy for hospitality, relational connection, or counseling as we have seen God use numerous strategies. We are insisting that you have a strategy for meeting people at the point of weakness. Not pursuing hearts at a moment when people are most likely to be transformed is a failure of leadership. Prepare the culture of your ministry to receive and minister to people while they are in a vulnerable posture.

Living the Words

After the research and biblical analysis formed the transformational discipleship framework, we outlined the book. As we began this important chapter, we were all confronted again with our own weakness.

While working on the book, I (Eric) left my role as executive pastor of Christ Fellowship to serve at LifeWay Christian Resources. The first month was painful, not because of anything wrong with the new role or the people but because everything was changing. The people I worked with for years were no longer surrounding me, my regular rhythm was disturbed, and I felt exposed and vulnerable. Honestly, I no longer felt "needed." The church I left was doing great . . . without me. And the division I was moving into was operating fine . . . without me.

God reminded me that He needs me for absolutely nothing. And in that reminder I experienced His grace and love. He does not need me, but because of His grace, He continually invites me to join Him in service to others. He brought me, once again, to the liberating realization of my own fragility and inadequacies. But in those moments He simultaneously refreshed my heart with His love for me.

While preparing to write this chapter, I (Philip) experienced one of the more traumatic moments of my life. My family and I were walking out to our car after a Sunday worship service when I lost the ability to speak for a short period of time.

> *He does not need me, but because of His grace, He continually invites me to join Him in service to others.*

After four tests at the hospital, the neurologists discovered I had suffered a ministroke due to a collapsed carotid artery. With no explanation as to why it happened, I was discharged and given blood thinner medications. The doctors hope the artery will heal within six months.

Every couple of weeks I have my INR levels checked (the chemicals that regulate blood clotting). If my blood is too thick, I could suffer a full-blown stroke. If my blood is too thin, it could seep into other systems of my body and cause infections. Though I can be grumpy from the weakness that goes with my condition and medication, I'm learning to stay in a posture of gratitude and humility. Every day is a reminder that life is brief and the unexpected can change everything in an instant. But every day is also a gift in which I can love my wife, raise my sons, and jump into the middle of God's mission.

I (Michael) am working on this chapter with my calendar pulled up beside the document. On that calendar there is a regular appointment on a Wednesday that now occurs every eight weeks. It's the day I take my seven-year-old son to the hematologist to make sure the cancer he was diagnosed with when he was two is still in remission.

Every eight weeks, and almost always more frequently than that, I'm reminded just how little I actually have control of in this life. I can't even protect my son, whom I love more than my life. In those moments I can either choose to despair, or I can choose once again to be reminded of the providential love and care of God who controls everything from the track of a tsunami to the white blood cell count in my little boy's body.

Weakness is not just for the people we serve. It is for us too. We need to treat it as the opportunity to experience God's transforming work. It is a friend to walk with us while God is strengthening us through the power of the gospel.

8
Interdependent

Sin demands to have a man by himself.
It withdraws him from the community.
The more isolated a person is, the more destructive
will be the power of sin over him.
—Dietrich Bonheoffer[1]

JUST NORTH OF SAN FRANCISCO is Muir Woods, an incredible forest that causes all who venture there to stand in awe of the strength and endurance of the sequoia trees. The sequoia trees are sometimes referred to as the largest living things on earth, reaching almost 250 feet in the air and standing for as many as fifteen hundred years.

When you stand before them, you feel tiny and envious at the same time. If you could have a conversation with one, you would be wise to ask: "How have you done it? How have you stood strong through all the storms of life, all the difficult situations? How have you not toppled?"

Their response, if they could speak, would be surprising.

The sequoia tree would not point to deep roots as the fundamental reason for standing strong through the centuries, as each tree's roots grow only about four feet in the ground. While there is nothing wrong with a continual insistence to "go deeper," the sequoia you stand like a dwarf before has not overcome the difficulties of life because of its depth.

His response would be to point to the other sequoias surrounding him, supporting him and keeping him strong. If you looked around, you would notice that sequoia trees grow only in groves. While their roots go only about four feet deep into the ground, their roots intermingle with the other sequoias next to them. Each tree is able to stand strong through the centuries because each tree has an interdependent posture.

No sequoia grows alone.

No believer is transformed alone.

Many church circles are experiencing a revival of "personal spiritual disciplines" that help believers encounter the grace of God. Moreover, the multitude of resources provided to Christians for "personal spiritual growth" is constantly on the rise, while simultaneously some church leaders are experimenting with "personal spiritual growth plans" for members, customized to the individual's learning style and current assessment of his spiritual life.

While we are grateful for the encouragement, resources, and opportunities for individuals to grow, we fear that the beauty and necessity of community may be lost. If a relationally vulnerable posture is abandoned, the resources may fill minds while not transforming hearts.

While interviews with believers who are being transformed revealed a posture of weakness to be absolutely essential for spiritual maturation, the discipleship leaders we interviewed overwhelmingly declared that transformation best occurs when a believer is in an interdependent posture with other believers. They were deeply concerned that the timeless truth of maturation in community is subtly being replaced with an American individualistic approach to spiritual growth that constantly promises roots that go deeper without roots that widen into relationships that intermingle. Because transformation occurs when a disciple is in an interdependent posture, discipleship leaders must slaughter individualism rather than celebrate it.

Aubrey Malphurs has given leadership to churches and church planting for decades. In discussing discipleship, he spoke of the need for our discipleship to emulate the relationship Jesus had with the early disciples. He said, "We look at them [the disciples], and they were really a struggling crew, but He [Jesus] took time out to relate to

> *Discipleship leaders must slaughter individualism rather than celebrate it.*

them." In discussing the constant neediness of the early believers, he described Jesus in this way: "So for example, we see His dealings with the disciples and how they keep falling flat, yet He picks them up and keeps going." Malphurs, throughout the interview, emphasized how we the church are to imitate the manner of Christ with other believers.

Alton Garrison is the assistant superintendent of the Assemblies of God. When Philip interviewed him about the state of discipleship in North America, he spoke a lot about relationships in the church. He emphasized the need for accountability among believers or there would likely be disastrous results. He said, "If you don't have a good enough relationship with somebody that will walk into your life and correct you, you are an out-of-control train headed down the track, a wreck that's going to happen."

Luis Cesar from Mexico defined the work of transformational discipleship in this vein. "We believe that discipleship is communion, is relationship," he said. "Relationships are essential in the lives of disciples; moreover, I would even dare to say absolutely everything in the Christian life has to do with relationships."

"Inter-," Not "De-" or "In-"

Transformation is likely to occur when a believer has truth applied to his or her life while in an interdependent posture. An interdependent posture is vastly different from either a dependent or an independent posture. A dependent posture is unhealthy as the believer finds security and worth in another person rather than Christ. Dependence on another is a form of idolatry, finding ultimate fulfillment in someone other than God, and saddles the relationship with unrealistic expectations. Equally destructive is independence as the believer attempts to live his faith alone. Bonheoffer warned of both in his classic work *Life Together* :

Let him who cannot be alone, beware the community . . .

Let him who is not in community, beware of being alone.[2]

Throughout the biblical narrative, community is emphasized and commanded; it is never presented as optional. Many have a misconception that the Christian faith is private. The Christian faith is personal but never private. In fact, the more personal the faith is to a believer the less private that faith becomes. If a person claims his faith is private, he has adopted a view that is contrary to God's. From the development of Israel to the building of the church, He has always gathered His people into groups.

The nature of the word *church* in the New Testament dictates that the Christian faith is not private and that God designed maturation to occur in the context of interdependent relation-

> *The Christian faith is personal but never private.*

ships. The word for "church" in the original language is *ekklesia*. It is a compound Greek word from two words, *ek,* which means "out," and *kaleo,* which means "to call." *Church* literally means "the called out ones." The word is plural in nature indicating that believers are automatically called to Christ out of the world and placed into the community of faith.

Believers know the importance of building relationships is a critical attribute in transformational discipleship. It is natural to live out our faith in an environment of relationships. Seventy-four percent of believers agree (strongly or somewhat) with the statement, "I have developed significant relationships with people at my church." In fact, only 3 percent strongly disagreed. Further, a majority of believers agree with the statement, "I intentionally try to get to know new people I meet at church." The development of relationships was evident in the lives of the believers surveyed.

Jesus cares deeply that His followers live with an interdependent posture in community with other Christ followers. In the hours leading up to His arrest, Jesus begged the Father to make His disciples one. He prayed:

> I pray not only for these, but also for those who believe
> in Me through their message. May they all be one, as
> You, Father, are in Me and I am in You. May they also
> be one in Us, so the world may believe You sent Me. I
> have given them the glory You have given Me. May they

be one as We are one. I am in them and You are in Me.
(John 17:20–23)

Jesus' prayer is a huge statement of His intention for those who claim to be His followers. He desires for His people to be as unified as He and the Father. The triune God is a community of three persons: Father, Son, and Holy Spirit. God who exists in community designed His followers to live in community for their maturity and to reflect His character.

How does an interdependent posture position someone for transformation? Why is community so vital to transformational discipleship?

Community Perfects

The apostle Paul wrote a passage concerning the process of spiritual maturity, or what theologians call "progressive sanctification:"

> I give thanks to my God for every remembrance of
> you, always praying with joy for all of you in my every
> prayer, because of your partnership in the gospel from
> the first day until now. I am sure of this, that He who
> started a good work in you will carry it on to completion
> until the day of Christ Jesus. (Phil. 1:3–6)

The context for Paul's certainty and confidence that God will continue the good work He began in the believers is the reality that they are in community together. While God is the one who is progressively perfecting the Christians living in Philippi (v. 6), God is using their partnership in the gospel (v. 4) to bring about Paul's transformation. The word for "partnership" in the original language is the Greek word *koinonia*, which is often translated *fellowship*. Paul believes in the power of God through community to transform.

When the first Christians responded to the gospel, they immediately threw themselves fully into partnership with one another. Acts 2:42 says, "They devoted themselves to the apostles' teaching, to the fellowship (*koinonia*)". *Koinonia* expresses participation, not just association. Transformational community is much deeper than mere association because of proximity. It is shared partnership for spiritual growth.

An interdependent posture is more than merely attending a small group or Sunday school class. Attending an environment designed for interdependence while refusing vulnerability and transparency will not put a believer in a transformative posture. Both the leader and the environment must welcome vulnerability without fostering dependence, knowing that both independence and dependence are the enemies of interdependence.

> *Discipleship is simply helping someone find and follow Jesus.*

We interviewed Steve Murrell as one of the experts in the area of discipleship. In 1984, Steve (a Caucasian from the U.S.) moved to the enormous city of Manila in the Philippines to plant a church. Today he pastors Victory Church that has an attendance of more than fifty thousand and has eighteen campuses around the city. In getting a definition from Steve about discipleship, he had a preference for keeping it simple. He stated the following:

I'd break it down to three aspects. It's following Jesus. It's fishing for people. And it's doing that in conjunction with others, in fellowship with others. Discipleship is simply helping someone find and follow Jesus. Helping someone

live out relationships with the lost, fishing for men, and
helping someone do that in community with others. And
if someone, if Matthew wanted to be a disciple of Jesus,
he had to do that along with Peter and James and the
others. So there was that fellowship issue. That's as simple
as I can get on it.

At his church they discuss disciple-making by the Four *Es*:
engage, establish, equip, and empower. Throughout the entire process, relationships are vital. In fact, at Victory Church, discipleship
does not occur outside of personal relationships.

Community Protects

When the author of Hebrews challenged believers to stand
firm and continue in the faith, he pointed to the necessity of interdependence and encouragement.

Watch out, brothers, so that there won't be in any of you
an evil, unbelieving heart that departs from the living
God. But encourage each other daily, while it is still
called today, so that none of you is hardened by sin's
deception. (Heb. 3:12–13)

Interdependence in community is as an antibiotic for sin's
deception. In our TD research, we observed that these believers
expect their Christian friends to challenge them when unwise
choices were made.

Martin Seligamen's research in the 1960s on "learned helplessness" is still widely respected among psychologists. Seligamen and
his team placed a dog in a cage designed to give electric shocks.
When they hit the cage with a jolt of electricity, the dog jumped
and yelped as expected. They waited a few minutes and shocked

the cage again, and the dog repeated the jumping and yelping. But after several shocks something strange happened; the dog responded less and less as he was completely hardened to the impact of the shock. The researchers opened the door to the cage and shocked the dog, hypothesizing that the dog would leave the cage when he was shocked. But the dog stayed in the cage; he was numb to the point of complacency and learned helplessness.

In the same way sin hardens and leaves even believers deceived and trapped while the door to the cage is wide open. The old cliché is true:

> Sin will take you further than you want to go, keep you
> longer than you want to stay, and cost you more than you
> want to pay.

The researchers continued their experiment by involving another dog, a dog not hardened by the electric shock and the learned helplessness of the cage. The researchers walked the new dog into the cage, and then they jolted the cage with an electric shock. The new dog jumped and yelped as he ran quickly out of the cage.

The first dog, seeing there was a better way to live, quickly followed to the freedom that was already his.

Interdependence is protection from sin's deceit. In the last chapter of Hebrews, the writer says simply, "Let brotherly love continue" (Heb. 13:1). The verse is extremely short as "brotherly love" is one word in the original language—*philadelphia*.

Philadelphia is composed of two root words: *phileo*, which means "brotherly love," and *adelphos*, which means "of the same womb." Thus philadelphia is a deep brotherly love for someone who has been born from the same womb. Believers have been born from the same God and must continue to love one another deeply so that sin does not deceive and harden.

It is safe to write that the YouTube clip "Battle at Krueger" has more viewers than this book will have readers as more than sixty-three million people have watched the clip. In the amateur clip filmed on a safari, viewers see a living example of community that protects. A herd of buffaloes are grazing in a field as several lions prowl at a distance, looking to see whom they may devour. The lions run after the buffaloes and take down the one who appears to be the weakest and slowest, a young calf. The scene is a bit grueling to watch, and things only get worse as the lions hold the young buffalo near a watering hole. At that point a crocodile comes out of the pond, grabs hold of the buffalo, and attempts to drag him into the water.

Life often feels the same, painful and difficult from multiple directions.

As the video continues, the lions wrestle the buffalo away from the crocodile, and the ending does not look promising . . . until the camera view widens. As the camera shot expands, the herd of buffaloes comes into full view. They are returning en masse to protect and defend their fallen comrade. No buffalo left behind! In epic fashion they chase the lions away and rescue their own. Community is the buffaloes's greatest defense from the merciless predators, both the seen (lions) and the unseen (crocodiles).

> *Christian community is supernatural but not always spectacular.*

Christian community is supernatural but not always spectacular. Sometimes the discussions in "community groups" are not as lively as they could be, at times the relationships don't thrive as we want them to do, and the people we are interdependently woven to are always normal and broken just as we are. Ministry and church leaders must quit promising spectacular community and instead offer the normal and messy because the normal and messy community is supernatural and transformational over time.

Community Preaches

The Super Bowl in 2002 featured the Saint Louis Rams and the New England Patriots. The Patriots were huge underdogs as the Rams were the ones with the high-powered offense that routinely racked up points against their opponents. The Patriots, many believed, were just lucky to be in the game. As the Super Bowl began, each team was asked to choose either their offense or defense to be introduced. Players dreamed of this moment, the opportunity for your name to be announced, from childhood games on empty lots and open streets.

As expected, the Rams chose their offensive starters to be introduced. And one by one each player ran unto the field to the sound of his own name. Some jogged slowly, savoring the moment. Others danced through the tunnel of cheerleaders. The Patriots' introductions followed, and their introductions were different from the Rams. ESPN commentator Trey Wingo called it "the coolest thing I have ever seen in thirty-six years of Super Bowl history." The crowd at the game and the viewing audience spread throughout thousands of Super Bowl parties noticed a stark contrast in the Patriots' introduction from that of the Rams.

And choosing to be introduced as a team, the New England Patriots.

Players sacrificed the honor of having their names broadcast to millions of viewers for the opportunity to display their unity. People stood in awe as the team ran onto the field as one, fans cried, and the announcers were speechless (a minor miracle in and of itself). The Patriots upset the Rams to win their first Super Bowl and were recognized as a team truly united in mission and purpose.

Community is always attractive; it always grabs the hearts of those who observe. Jesus promised that the world would understand the gospel because of the love and unity of believers (John 13:35; 17:23). From a missiological standpoint Christian community is a statement of the gospel in the culture.

In the church and in the community, as we see people through the lens of the gospel, we will be transformed into servants rather than those waiting to be served. The transformation brought about by the Holy Spirit will guide us to demonstrate His effect on our lives. The TD research continuously found the pattern that Christians understand the need to serve both God and others as a part of their discipleship. To the statement, "I regularly find myself meeting a need without being asked," 60 percent strongly or somewhat agreed. The research found an even higher majority (68 percent agreement) to the statement, "I am intentionally putting my spiritual gift(s) to use serving God and others."

> **Christian community is a statement of the gospel in the culture.**

We are recognized as His not by our cool music, programs, vision statements, facilities, or even our evangelistic zeal. We are known as His by our unity. Therefore the end result of authentic Christian community is not community itself but mission. Ultimately the world surrounding the community is impacted by how God works within the community of believers.

Broken Buzzwords

Because believers are likely to grow when in an interdependent posture, ministry leaders must value authentic community that perfects, protects, and preaches. But as we long to foster community, "community" has often become a broken buzzword, and we must move beyond the buzzwords to helping people experience the interdependent community Jesus prayed for and desires. While we love the word *community* because of its basic meaning, the word has been used to describe anything and everything a ministry does, so sadly it often describes nothing. Community must be more than a nebulous term casually placed on anything a ministry offers. In short, leaders must not only cast a vision for community but must also define the values of community in a given context.

And while we appreciate the word *organic* because we love the thought of ministry leaders creating such a healthy culture that biblical community just happens organically, the word is often thrown up as an excuse for unintentional discipleship. "Uh. Hmmm. Uh. It just sort of happens. Organically." "Organic" growth must be the result of a healthy culture created by sound teaching and leadership and not a spiritual tag we apply to all things done haphazardly.

Community literally means "common unity"; therefore, a community is a group of people united around a common belief system, set of values, and mission. This is the essence of Paul's challenge to "fulfill my joy by thinking the same way, sharing the same feelings, focusing on one goal" (Phil. 2:2). The strength of community is only as strong as the strength of what brings people together. Robert Coleman said that the ministry done for one another is "the glue that holds discipleship together."

> Community literally means "common unity."

Since the community Jesus envisioned flows from unity with Him *(May they also be one in Us?)* and a commitment to those not yet His *(that the world will know)*, leaders must build community around the truth of Jesus and His mission. Since unity is strongest when fostered around values that are rock solid, unity must be built on the common commitment to the character of God and His mission. Or leaders can seek to unite people around anything and foster weak community because of a shaky set of shared beliefs and values.

For the sake of transformation, the people in your ministry must live interdependently with other believers; you must nudge people to live in community. But how? How does a leader teach and shepherd someone to a place of interdependence, not merely attending a program designed for community? Let's return to the three lenses from which wise discipleship leaders view truth. The truth is that the people you are responsible for need to abandon the lie of a private faith and live in community, and the three lenses serve as motivators for interdependence.

Gospel and Community

Christian community is a beautiful reflection of the gospel. In fact, community only exists because of the gospel. D. A. Carson writes:

> [The church] is made up of natural enemies. What binds us together is not common education, common race, common income levels, common politics, common nationality, common accents, common jobs, or anything else of that sort. Christians come together . . . because they have all been saved by Jesus Christ. . . . They are a

band of natural enemies who love one another for Jesus' sake.[3]

When the apostle Paul wrote the church in Philippi (Phil. 1:3–6) about their partnership *(koinonia)* in the gospel, he wrote a diverse group of believers who were only in community because of the gospel; their partnership existed because Christ had rescued them and placed them in community.

> *Their partnership existed because Christ had rescued them and placed them in community.*

Acts 16 gives a snapshot of several of the individuals who formed the community Paul wrote about in his letter to the church at Philippi.[4] One of them is a woman named Lydia who was a dealer in purple cloth, a prominent and savvy businesswoman. After she received Christ, she immediately persuaded Paul and his companions to stay at her house while they shared the gospel in Philippi. Another in the community is a former slave girl who was used by her owners to make money by telling people their future through an evil spirit that possessed her. Another in the community was the prison guard who was on duty when Paul and Silas prayed and sang their way out of their shackles.

The small group consisted of a wealthy businesswoman, a slave girl, and a blue-collar jailer—all rescued by the power of the gospel. They gathered together, read the Scripture together, encouraged one another, and prayed for one another. People on the outside of the faith looked at the diverse group who walked into Lydia's house for their meetings and surely thought things looked a bit odd. They probably did not frequent the same restaurants, listen to the same music, or enjoy the same hobbies; but something much greater than their music preference, restaurant selection, or place of residence united them. Because God had radically transformed them, they had a bond that was deeper than anything that could divide them—the same glorious gospel.

Believers do not simply gather for random get-togethers. Though they enjoy being with one another, the TD research showed that factors like gathering for Bible study, praying together, praying for church leaders, and participating in regular responsibilities with the church were all indicative of spiritual growth. We see from the Scriptures, and in the intent of today's believers, that joining together for service, worship, study, and mentoring lead to spiritual transformation.

When we live in community with other believers, we reflect the gospel because Christ has made us one. Because of the gospel, we enjoy partnership with God and one another. Leaders who employ the gospel motivation for community challenge believers to live in community that is formed on the gospel and not on other uniting factors. Groups filled with people that are similar in socioeconomic status, profession, education, or culture must particularly be challenged for the gospel to be the chief uniting factor, the foundation of first importance. The challenge must be consistent because groups with other uniting similarities easily drift to weaker community formed on issues other than the gospel.

Discipline and Community

The Scriptures are loaded with instructions for how believers should interact and live in an interdependent community. These exhortations are often called the "one another" commands, and their number makes them impossible to miss:

- Love one another. (John 13:34)
- Show family affection to one another. (Rom. 12:10)

- Be in agreement with one another. (Rom. 12:16)
- Accept one another. (Rom. 15:7)
- Instruct one another. (Rom. 15:14)
- Greet one another. (Rom. 16:16)
- Serve one another. (Gal. 5:13)
- Be kind and compassionate to one another, forgiving each other, just as God also forgave you in Christ. (Eph. 4:32)
- Submit to one another out of reverence for Christ. (Eph. 5:21)
- Admonish one another with all wisdom. (Col. 3:16)
- Encourage one another and build each other up. (1 Thess. 5:11)
- Be hospitable to one another. (1 Pet. 4:9)
- Confess your sins to one other and pray for one other. (James 5:16)

When a leader understands the spiritual disciplines as putting the believer in the right posture to be transformed, these instructions are understood as essentials for a healthy, Christ-centered community of believers, which is transformational for those who belong. The "one another" commands cannot be lived in isolation; they must be lived with "one another."

Identity and Community

The Scriptures give several metaphors describing the beauty of Christian community and the interdependent relationships God graciously gives. Because Christians are children of God, fellow believers are brothers and sisters in Christ in the family of God who are to "show family affection to one another." Believers also make up the body of Christ (Rom. 12:4–5), where all the members are necessary and belong to all the others.

Ministry leaders who view discipleship, in part, through the lens of identity and desire to see believers in a posture of interdependence challenge believers to live out what it means to be a member of a greater body and a brother or sister in Christ. These leaders remind believers that to be disconnected is to betray what God declares your position in the greater family to be.

The sequoia tree is still standing because its roots are connected. It lives in an interdependent community. The people you serve who are not in a posture of interdependence are in deep jeopardy of toppling.

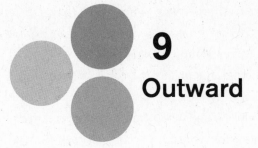

9
Outward

Every Christian is either a missionary or an impostor.
—Charles Spurgeon[1]

THE NATION OF GEORGIA is bordered to the west by the Black Sea and the north by Russia. The central region is hill country, but a landmark sticks out like a sore thumb from the landscape. The Katskhi Pillar is a rock formation that rises more than 130 feet from the hills below and resembles a giant's club.

Because of its unique appearance, especially set against the backdrop of its surroundings, the pillar was considered a pagan holy site for a long time and was most likely used in the worship practices of fertility gods. But in the fourth century Georgia adopted Christianity as its state religion, and the fertility rites began to fade away. As it did, worship at the Katskhi Pillar transitioned to the new belief system along with the rest of the country.

In the seventh century a small church was built on top of the rock formation.

A man (no women are allowed to the top) can still ascend the creaky ladder, known as the stairway to heaven by the locals, and worship in the church. They might even meet the Georgian monk who has been living there for more than twenty years.

As strange as the placement of the church or ascending the ladder to worship there might seem, the effort it took to build a structure on top of the pillar is emblematic of the practice of a group of Christian ascetics who have become known as Stylites. The word comes from the Greek *stylos*, meaning "pillar," and describes Christians who, in the fifth century, were known to stand on pillars preaching, fasting, and praying. They believed that living on top of these pillars was the best means of crucifying the flesh and therefore growing in discipleship. The first such Stylite was probably a man called Simeon who was said to have climbed a pillar in Syria in 423 and stayed there until he died. *About forty years later.*

While we might scoff at the suggestion of living our lives seated on a pillar, the spirit behind such actions rings true with us at some level. We know, of course that a disciple of Christ cannot "love the world or the things that belong to the world. If anyone loves the world, love for the Father is not in him" (1 John 2:15). Paul certainly was a proponent of putting to death everything that belongs to the worldly nature (Col. 3:5), and Jesus advocated going to great lengths to avoid sin:

> If your hand or foot causes your downfall, cut it off and
> throw it away. It is better for you to enter life maimed
> or lame, than to have two hands or two feet and be
> thrown into the eternal fire. And if your eye causes your

downfall, gouge it out and throw it away. It is better for
you to enter life with one eye, rather than to have two
eyes and be thrown into hellfire! (Matt. 18:8–9)

Passages like these make you want to climb a pillar. Or if not
climb one physically, to have the same sort of mentality where
you can completely separate from the world. There aren't many
churches in the world that so literally take this desire to separate
from the world that they're willing to build a structure 140 feet in
the air, but there are plenty who live with that mentality.

That mentality is one of the driving forces behind the attempt
to create a Christianized version of every part of society—school,
music, literature, T-shirts, candy—in order that those inside might
be protected from the influence of those outside. In the spirit of
passages like James 1:27, which qualifies "true religion" in part as
keeping "oneself unstained by the world," the benchmark for true
discipleship is the lack of the presence of the world.

We are figuratively, if not physically, living on pillars.

Defense or Offense?

So what's the big deal about living on pillars? It seems from
the passages above that there's some pragmatic value to it. You're
not going to be easily polluted by the world if all of the temptation
is 140 feet below. If that's true, then, we must think that part of
the posture of transformational discipleship is an element of
separation . . . right?

One issue with this posture of discipleship is that it assumes
evil and wickedness come from without. By living on a pillar, then,
you effectively remove temptation. But anyone who has pursued
godliness for more than about five minutes knows the fallacy

of that thinking. The pull of the flesh is too strong. The lure of sin is too great. And even on that pillar, such is the state of the human heart that we will be drawn into sin. Jesus' exhortations in particular remind us that the evil isn't just "out there"; the evil is "in here."

What was causing the sin in Matthew 18 that had to be so drastically dealt with? It was a hand. An eye. A part of a person rather than an outside influence. Greed, pride, lust, anger—you can't escape these desires on a pillar, for even on the pillar you still have "you" to deal with.

Another issue with this posture is that although Jesus, Paul, and James said the things recorded above, those aren't the only things they said. Jesus, while He commanded extreme measures in dealing with sin, also specifically prayed against this kind of pillar-like existence: "I am not praying that You take them out of the world but that You protect them from the evil one" (John 17:15). And then further: "As You sent Me into the world, I also have sent them into the world" (John 17:18). Jesus doesn't send His disciples onto pillars; He sends them into the thick of battle. Angel Mena Garcia with the Assemblies of God in Panama described his ministry this way: "Our obligation as pastors is to teach and train members, so in any context of life they can also share in the evangelism. I don't consider myself a desk pastor; I am a pastor of the street."

> *I don't consider myself a desk pastor; I am a pastor of the street.*

When you live your life on a pillar, you are taking a primarily defensive posture. You are fighting back every potential evil influence from yourself, your home, your kids. These influences assail you at every turn, but the mature disciple knows how to keep his or her weapons at the ready to make sure no one or nothing climbs up on that pillar.

Jesus' design for the life of the disciple is not one of defense; it's one of offense. Consider the way Jesus described the church, right after Peter's confession of Him as the true Messiah, the Son of God: "And I also say to you that you are Peter, and on this rock I will build My church, and the forces of Hades will not overpower it. I will give you the keys of the kingdom of heaven, and whatever you bind on earth is already bound in heaven, and whatever you loose on earth is already loosed in heaven" (Matt. 16:18–19). True enough, there is a defensive component in these verses. The church will be able to stand against the attacks of the enemy, but this passage is dominated with offensive language. The church is the keeper

> *Jesus' design for the life of the disciple is not one of defense; it's one of offense.*

of the keys of heaven and is given extraordinary power. This is power to take the fight to the ends of the earth, not just adequately defend itself.

Engaged Not Reactive

The same sentiment is echoed in Jesus' marching orders to His followers: "Go, therefore, and make disciples of all nations, baptizing them in the name of the Father and of the Son and of the Holy Spirit, teaching them to observe everything I have commanded you. And remember, I am with you always, to the end of the age" (Matt. 28:19–20). Jesus assumes an offensive posture in these verses. The verb tense here indicates a perpetual state of motion, an "always going," and, as that going happens, a commitment to the spread of the gospel to every nation, tongue, and people.

James, who made sure his readers understood that pure religion involved keeping oneself from being polluted by the world, also wrote some of the strongest commands in the entire canon about involvement in the world. In as much as pure religion is keeping oneself from worldly pollution, it's also "to look after orphans and widows in their distress" (James 1:27). This is offensive language, a call to believers to be actively involved in the world around them.

Paul got in on the act, too. After reminding the Ephesians to "be imitators of God, as dearly loved children" (Eph. 5:1), he spoke more specifically about how that is accomplished: "Pay careful attention, then, to how you walk—not as unwise people but as wise—making the most of the time, because the days are evil" (Eph. 5:15–16).

Now at first glance it seems that Paul is advocating a defensive sort of carefulness. Because the days are so evil, be careful where you step; you don't want to get any sin on your shoes. So you defensively tiptoe through life, being always careful. It's the kind of carefulness that I (Michael) use in my own home when I check on our three kids late at night.

We live in a house built in the late 1950s, and because it still has the original floors, there is a lot of creaking as you walk. So when I go up the stairs to their rooms, I have to be careful where I walk. I have to watch closely every footfall because I know that with one misstep they are going to wake up. Then who knows what will happen.

But this isn't the kind of carefulness Paul is advocating. You know it's not because of the link to verse 1. If that verse sets off this section of application, then everything is framed around his opening exhortation to be imitators of God. And God plays offense.

He speaks and nothing becomes something.

He sets in motion a plan to bring His people from bondage.

He attacks the idolatry of the land through the armies of His people.

And through it all, He is working on His plan formed before the creation of the world to take the initiative to redeem sinners through Jesus Christ.

God plays offense. He's not caught off guard, never once surprised. There is no such thing as a Plan B with God. He is never reactive. If we are to imitate Him, we are to not to be tippy-toeing through life. We are to walk boldly through the world, making sure we miss no opportunity to do good for the sake of the gospel.

> *We are to walk boldly through the world.*

The carefulness in this passage isn't meant to cause us to cower back; it's meant to make us anxious, always looking around us for any chance we see for good. Earl Creps said in our interview, "I think that mission is kind of a piece of whole cloth that covers my house, my community, and the world all at the same time." In this, we literally "redeem" the time given to us. We buy it back from the evil that so dominates it. But because our time is limited to do so, we must be careful not to miss any opportunity in our homes, schools, workplaces, grocery stores, gas stations, and anywhere else we walk.

A disciple of Jesus, then, is someone who walks with his or her head on a swivel, constantly looking for these opportunities to push back the darkness and let in the light. In order to live with that kind of carefulness, you must have an outward-facing posture.

Taking the Fight to the World

If Jesus wanted us in a morally and ministry neutral position, we would be commanded to get on a pillar. Instead, disciples being transformed are ones who are moving forward. Our research found that 80 percent of believers are praying for the unsaved at least once a month (21 percent doing so daily). Beyond prayer a majority of believers had also been seeking to involve the unchurched in worship services within six months of participating in the survey.

Certainly, as the gospel is the key to our redemption and growth, we want to see believers actively engaging in conversations about it. And many are. Almost three-quarters agreed with the statement, "I feel comfortable that I can share my belief in Christ with someone else effectively" (31 percent strongly and 43 agree somewhat). It is the impulse we need to see if Christians are to live an outward-facing life.

But to do so means they are unashamed of Christ and His gospel, even when the world disapproves. And the world will disapprove. Believers today are going public with their faith. When posed with the negative statement, "Many people who know me are not aware I am a Christian," 72 percent disagreed (37 percent strongly and 35 percent somewhat). Another negative statement posed to believers was, "I am hesitant to let others know that I am a Christian." A total of 83 percent disagreed, with 57 percent strongly disagreeing. The degree of separation from these types of attitudes is a good indicator that maturing believers are proudly displaying their faith in both word and action.

All of this helps encourage us that believers want to live in such a way that others are well aware of Christ and His impact on their lives. It is a signal that the body of Christ wants to make our faith public. As growth occurs, it inclines the believer to share what has transformed him or her. Rather than huddle, groups of believers

> *Rather than cower, we should go on the offensive.*

mobilize. Rather than cower, we should go on the offensive. But at times we seem to stutter-step.

Obstacles to Facing Out

Comfort

Even the early church, many of whom were there when Jesus promised them power and commissioned them to be sent out, struggled with living outwardly. Though in Acts 1:8 they were clearly instructed to have this outward focus, taking the gospel through the power of the Spirit, to an ever-widening area until they reached the ends of the earth, they stayed put.

Pentecost came, the Spirit fell, the church grew, and they stayed put.

Miracles happened, the lame walked, more sermons were preached, and they stayed put.

More miracles happened, deacons were chosen, more sermons were preached, and they stayed put. The Jerusalem part of Acts 1:8 was in full swing, but no one was going out. The lure of the pillar is strong.

But just when the fledgling church might have been facing the temptation to turn completely inward, to choose seclusion, Stephen was tragically martyred, and "on that day a severe persecution broke out against the church in Jerusalem, and all except the apostles were scattered throughout the land of Judea and Samaria" (Acts 8:1).

The pull to inward focus is so strong that it took a dramatic falling of violence and oppression to force the believers to begin to move forward in the Acts 1:8 directive. What is so appealing about living on that pillar? What makes it so difficult to have a true outward focus as a disciple?

Ease

Some of the answers are easier than others. Honestly, it's just easier. It's certainly safer because there's so little contact and potential confrontation with the outside world. On the pillar there is an element of control you can feel (albeit an illusion). And then there's the plain and simple fact that in our fallen nature we tend to be self-preservationists. We think primarily of ourselves from when we are newly born babies.

Pride

There is a more sinister reason we struggle with an outward focus: pride. It is one of the more destructive reasons an outward-focused life is avoided. As a disciple, "life on the pillar" might seem, from an outside observer's point of view, a showing of true humility. But pride rears its ugly head in a number of ways. Sure, there's the obvious ways pride manifests itself in terms of a massive ego, people who can't be pleased by anyone else and insist on their way all the time in every detail. But then there are the more subtle forms.

False humility, for example, is really just another form of pride. People who continually beat their chest, constantly berating themselves for their sinfulness to the point of paralysis are, in the end, just as prideful as those who think they are God's gift to mankind. In the end both are truly focused on themselves—one is focused on how bad they are while the other is focused on how good.

Keep in mind, though, that people following Jesus—really following Jesus—have their eyes fixed on Him. The writer of Hebrews reminds us:

> Therefore, since we also have such a large cloud of
> witnesses surrounding us, let us lay aside every weight
> and the sin that so easily ensnares us. Let us run with

endurance the race that lies before us, keeping our eyes on Jesus, the source and perfecter of our faith, who for the joy that lay before Him endured a cross and despised the shame and has sat down at the right hand of God's throne. (Heb. 12:1–2)

It's interesting that the writer wants us to throw off sin *and* every weight that might slow us down in this race. Every weight, then, is something other than sin. Perhaps in this case it's self-focus. When you're running a race, your eyes are fixed on the finish line. You are so fixed on the goal that you have little time to look at anything else.

> *When you're running a race, your eyes are fixed on the finish line.*

Perspective Leads to Action

An outward focus requires a true form of humility, which isn't come to, as C. S. Lewis famously said, by thinking less of yourself but by thinking of yourself less. Easier said than done though, right?

How do people think of themselves less? Certainly not by sheer will. If you try to think of yourself less, you'll only find that you're thinking of yourself more—you're thinking about how to make yourself think less of yourself! No, the only real way is to look to something so beautiful, so captivating, so wonderful that your full attention and affection are focused there.

No one stands at the rim of the Grand Canyon and thinks about how great they are. No one stares into the billions of stars in the sky and considers their own importance. When you are confronted with true greatness, you fix your attention there.

You think less of yourself by pondering, over and over again, Jesus. His life, death, and resurrection. The gospel, over and over again. This is the spirit behind the early Christian hymn Paul recorded for us in Philippians 2 when he urged his readers to make their attitude like that of Christ Jesus,

> Who, existing in the form of God, did not consider equality with God as something to be used for His own advantage. Instead He emptied Himself by assuming the form of a slave, taking on the likeness of men. And when He had come as a man in His external form, He humbled Himself by becoming obedient to the point of death— even to death on a cross. For this reason God highly exalted Him and gave Him the name that is above every name, so that at the name of Jesus every knee will bow— of those who are in heaven and on earth and under the earth—and every tongue should confess that Jesus Christ is Lord, to the glory of God the Father. (Phil. 2:6–11)

An outward focus requires that we look to Jesus as our focal point, not just merely as a good example. The imagination-capturing, awe-inspiring Son of God is more than enough to hold our gaze. And when we feel it wandering somewhere else, we must refocus on Him again and again.

Interestingly, as we focus on Jesus more passionately, we will increasingly focus on others as well. Notice what Paul said just before this beautiful refrain about the beauty of Christ: "Do nothing out of rivalry or conceit, but in humility consider others as more important than yourselves. Everyone should look out not only

> *The imagination-capturing, awe-inspiring Son of God is more than enough to hold our gaze.*

for his own interests, but also for the interests of others" (Phil. 2:3–4).

Do you want to stop thinking about yourself? Look to Jesus.

Do you want to start thinking of others? Look to Jesus.

If you want to live an outwardly focused life, then look to Jesus again and again.

This tie between our worship of Jesus and our outward focus on those around us is evident throughout Scripture. As the early church learned more about all that had been done for them in the gospel, their focus shifted to Jesus, and they found themselves caring for others in a truly selfless way:

> Now all the believers were together and held all things
> in common. They sold their possessions and property
> and distributed the proceeds to all, as anyone had a need.
> Every day they devoted themselves to meeting together
> in the temple complex and broke bread from house to
> house. They ate their food with a joyful and humble
> attitude, praising God and having favor with all the
> people. And every day the Lord added to them those who
> were being saved. (Acts 2:44–47)

Jesus reiterated this by reminding the people of His day of the greatest commandments of all, the ones that sum up all the others: "Love the Lord your God with all your heart, with all your soul, and with all your mind. This is the greatest and most important command. The second is like it: Love your neighbor as yourself. All the law and the Prophets depend on these two commands" (Matt. 22:37–40).

The posture of the disciple is an outward-facing one. That makes all the sense in the world when we consider what the outward-facing disciple is looking to.

More Than a Project

The temptation is to try to force yourself and others into such a posture. We can manipulate ourselves into doing so through any number of means; guilt, obligation, bargaining are a few. But in the end our natural inclination is to turn inward. Only through seeing the greatness of Christ can we truly assume an outwardly focused posture.

But when that does happen, when we are captured by the wondrous beauty of the gospel, when our attention is fixed on Jesus and on others, we begin to see that this truly is a posture, not a project.

There's nothing wrong with projects. They can often be the catalyst for moving us into a greater sense of God's mission in the world. So we might dedicate a specific amount of time for the sake of God or for others. We might take an overseas mission trip, serve at a homeless shelter, or volunteer at an after-school tutoring program. Funny thing about projects, though—they are, by nature, short term. And more times than not, despite our best intentions, we find ourselves drifting back into an inward focus and posture once again. Or else we treat these projects like a quota system whereby we do our due diligence for the sake of the kingdom all at once so we don't have to worry about it again until next month, year, or decade.

There is a better way.

These projects, rather than being a way to quell our consciences, should rightly flow from a constant posture of focusing outward. That posture is the position of the disciple, and because he's positioned outwardly, every project engaged is merely a natural extension of everyday life.

Great idea, but how do you get to that point? How do you come to a point where you truly have an outward posture and so it's not unusual for you to engage in these specialized projects? One word is key here: *margin.*

A passage in Leviticus can help move us along toward an outward posture. Here the people of God are instructed in the way they are to plow their fields:

> **One word is key here: margin.**

> When you reap the harvest of your land, you are not to
> reap to the very edge of your field or gather the gleanings
> of your harvest. You must not strip your vineyard bare or
> gather its fallen grapes. Leave them for the poor and the
> foreign resident; I am Yahweh your God. (Lev. 19:9–10)

Here we see God telling His people a practical way to create margin in their lives. God is so concerned about the poor and the foreigners that He built a means into the regular life of His people to provide food for them. He made sure people didn't harvest all the way to the edges of the field. The edges were "just in case."

Just in case someone traveling needs food.

Just in case you have a chance to share with someone in need.

Just in case someone else needs to feed their family.

Just in case the leftovers can be useful after all for something other than giving you more.

See it? This command defies the constant call of our culture for "more." We live in a margin-less world. Our calendars are booked with meetings and appointments end to end. So are our pocket-books. In fact, everything from our time to our money is pretty much spoken for. We are plowing to the end of the fields. We are going back over the fields of our lives a second and third time, looking for any spare cent or second that has not been accounted for.

The way you integrate this command into your real life today is that in all these areas, you don't plow to the edge. You don't book meetings back to back in case there is a conversation God will bring your way. You don't spend all the way to the end of your paycheck in case there is an unforeseen chance to be generous. You don't overschedule your family with activity after activity so that there isn't a single second to spend with your neighbors in the yard.

Once again, though, the impetus behind this margin is the constant gaze on Jesus. When you are looking to Him, you will find that all the imperatives of life don't seem so imperative any more. And suddenly those edges of the fields you thought you needed, you find out can actually be set aside, creating room for others.

An outward posture leaves that kind of room at the edges, just in case. Having an outward focus requires teaching margin to those you lead, but to do so also requires teaching self-control and contentment. The virtues are needed in our mentality so that our outward perspective will result in missionary activity.

Think how history might have looked if an early Christian named Ananias had plowed all the way to the edges. Think if he hadn't had time to pray, seeking the face of the Lord. Think if he had an appointment booked when he got the message that he was needed to affirm the calling of a surprising person.

> *An outward posture leaves that kind of room at the edges.*

But Ananias had the margin. He hadn't plowed to the edges. Because he hadn't, he could get up and go across town when the Lord told him to:

"Get up and go to the street called Straight," the Lord said to him, "to the house of Judas, and ask for a man from Tarsus named Saul, since he is praying there. In a vision he has seen a man named Ananias coming in and placing his hands on him so he can regain his sight. . . . For this man is My chosen instrument to take My name to Gentiles, kings, and the Israelites." (Acts 9:11–12, 15)

Or consider what would have happened if Philip had been too busy to head down south of Jerusalem. Maybe he had double-booked himself again, perhaps with a couple of speaking engagements. But he hadn't plowed to the edges either, and because he hadn't, the gospel began to spread to Ethiopia (Acts 8:26–40).

Then there's the most literal example of all. During some dark days of Israel, days of great idolatry, there was still a man who took seriously the law of God and didn't plow to the edges. Because he didn't, a young widow named Ruth was able to glean the wheat from the edges in order to provide food for her and her mother-in-law, Naomi. Boaz, the owner of the field, ended up marrying the gleaner Ruth, and a few generations later comes Jesus Christ.

Great things can happen when you don't plow to the edges of your life. Ultimately faith can drive you to such a choice because you are consciously making an effort to choose less for some unknown reason. But what is "just in case" to us has divine meaning and purpose to God.

The three lenses of truth only serve to further the need for an outward posture in the life of the believer.

An Outward Posture and the Gospel

For Paul, believing the gospel led to an outward focus. The gospel doesn't ask but *compels* us out into the world: "For Christ's love compels us, since we have reached this conclusion: If One died for all, then all died" (2 Cor. 5:14). The gospel creates in us a new way to see people. Everyone is an eternal being now, either destined for eternal glory or eternal wrath. With this new vision comes a great responsibility. God has "committed the message of reconciliation to us. Therefore, we are ambassadors for Christ, certain that God is appealing through us. We plead on Christ's behalf, 'Be reconciled to God'" (2 Cor. 5:19–20).

The language here is telling. Ambassadors are those who live in foreign lands for the specific purpose of extending the interests of their homeland there. Though they might be on foreign soil, they still operate under the rule and law and principles of their true home. Can you think of a more appropriate way to explain what we are about here on earth?

Thanks to the gospel, our citizenship has been changed. We've got another home—another kingdom. But God has sent us into the kingdom of the world, while operating under the principles of our true kingdom, in order to extend His interests and glory here. An ambassador, by the nature of the job, has to have an outward posture. So do we as we plead with others to be reconciled to God.

> *An ambassador, by the nature of the job, has to have an outward posture.*

Leading others to have an outward posture will necessitate that we illustrate it with our own lives. If you are a pastor, teacher, staff member, or leader of any sort in the church, people need to see an outward focus from you on a personal level. The notorious reputation of pastors is that they tell everyone else to go and reach the world while they study about it in an office. Such a story should never be told of the leaders in our churches. Instead, we need to take believers with us as we have a barbecue in the neighborhood, meet with a city council member, or travel to some far-flung place on the globe.

An Outward Posture and Discipline

It seems counterintuitive to think about having an outward posture and practicing the spiritual disciplines. We think of the disciplines as inherently inwardly focused—these are the means by which we examine ourselves and deepen our knowledge and intimacy with Jesus. While that's true, an outward posture is associated with them as well. As a case study, consider the argument between God and His people recorded in Isaiah 58.

From the perspective of the people, God wasn't living up to His end of the bargain. They were religious—exceedingly religious in fact—so much so that they were seeking God day after day and seemed delighted to know His ways (Isa. 58:2). They were so committed that they were regularly fasting and afflicting themselves, going beyond the one day of prescribed fasting in the law on the Day of Atonement.

These people were masters of spiritual discipline, and yet in verse 1, God told Isaiah to "cry out loudly, don't hold back! Raise your voice like a trumpet. Tell My people their transgression and the house of Jacob their sins." As the chapter progresses, we find out the nature of the sin of the people despite their religious appearance.

Ironically, while these good folks were denying themselves food, people in their community were starving. Others were walking around without clothes and sleeping on the street. And God's point was simple: "What are you doing with all that food you're *not* eating? You might think about giving it to the people who are hungry."

The people were masters of self-deprivation, but God wanted more. He wanted an outward posture to their discipline. In all their spiritual zeal and commitment, God was reminding them not to forget about those around them. That's the kind of spiritual discipline He's after:

> Isn't the fast I choose: To break the chains of wickedness, to untie the ropes of the yoke, to set the oppressed free, and to tear off every yoke? Is it not to share your bread with the hungry, to bring the poor and homeless into your house, to clothe the naked when you see him, and not to ignore your own flesh and blood? (Isa. 58:6–7)

When you fast, what happens to the food? When you discipline yourself to say no to material things, what happens to the money? When you pray, what is the focus? These are questions we must ask ourselves. Leaders must ask them of their people.

An Outward Posture and Identity

Only through understanding how dramatically we have been changed in Christ can we be truly free to look outwardly. The Holy Spirit testifies time and time again with your own spirit that, regardless of what else happens in life, you are a child of God (Rom. 8:15–16). With His encouragement and application of the Scripture to your life, the Spirit will create a new sense of freedom in your life. This is particularly important when you consider the way in which we tend to "use" others rather than truly love them.

By our nature we want to be around people who make us feel better about ourselves. We work to surround ourselves with people who think we look nice, are eager to hear our ideas, and think everything we put on Facebook is worth repeating in person. These are your biggest fans, and because they are, you like to be around them.

Conversely, we also gather those who are "worse off" around us. Bad at handling money, poor morals, and not too bright—we like them around so we can seem to be the shining light in the room. We think inwardly that we are doing them a favor by associating with them, but the truth is that being around them makes us feel better about ourselves by way of comparison. We may be bad, but at least we're not as bad as "that guy."

Then there are the relationships we form under the guise of networking. We sidle up to someone of great importance, esteem, wealth, or power, and we like being there and breathing the same air they breathe. We feel more important by proxy because if we are around this type of person, we must have some value on our own.

In all these instances we are using these people for our own benefit. The need to use others comes from a plaguing sense of insecurity that is common to almost all of humanity. We all know at some level that we're frauds, and we hope no one else finds out the truth.

Only through the new identity in Christ—the one that comes to us by grace through faith and cannot be revoked or taken away—can the root of this insecurity be attacked. If we are fully accepted in Christ and have been made the sons and daughters of God, then suddenly we don't have to use those around us any more. Our personal identity and self-worth are established in and validated by the cross, and as we grow to believe more and more what the Bible says about us, we become free of the need of external markers of our identity.

> *Our personal identity and self-worth are established in and validated by the cross.*

We are free to have an outward posture, focusing on the good of others rather than what good they might bring to us. At long last we are free to love rather than to use.

The Means as Well as the Effect

From a leadership perspective, there is one other perception regarding an outward posture that is, by God's grace, beginning to change. For a long time this kind of outward posture was seen as the effect of discipleship. That is to say, when people finally reach a certain level of maturity, they are ready to engage in mission trips, service projects, and other extensions of an outward posture.

But facing outward isn't only the effect of discipleship; it's also the means of discipleship. Mary Kassian said, "I don't see discipleship just as a dissemination of information or even as just a relational interaction, but at heart it's also ministry."

While one of the marks of transformation is thinking less about self and more about God and others, actively pursuing that posture is also one of the means by which people grow as disciples. Paul didn't wait until he had sufficiently matured as a disciple to start preaching; he went out and started preaching to others: "Saul was with the disciples in Damascus for some days. Immediately he began proclaiming Jesus in the synagogues: 'He is the Son of God'" (Acts 9:19–20). Likewise, the disciples received the Holy Spirit and immediately got to work building the church in Acts 2. The pattern is not grow, then turn outward; it's grow by turning outward.

If that's true, then leaders must encourage their people as a means of discipleship to be actively involved in bringing the kingdom of God to bear on earth. What we'll find, then, is that God is indeed at work in us as much as He is at work through us.

Part 3

Transformational Framework: LEADERS

The Transformational Sweet Spot
is the intersection of truth given by healthy leaders
to someone in a vulnerable posture.

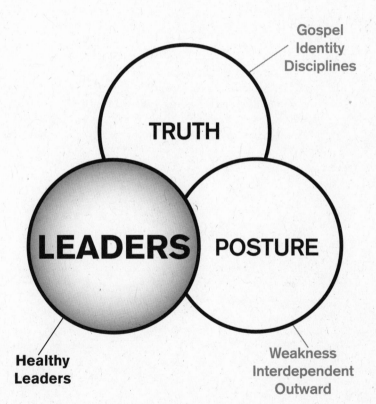

Gospel
Identity
Disciplines

TRUTH

LEADERS POSTURE

**Healthy
Leaders**

Weakness
Interdependent
Outward

*Jesus called them over and said, "You know
that the rulers of the Gentiles dominate them, and the
men of high position exercise power over them.
It must not be like that among you. On the contrary,
whoever wants to become great among you must be
your servant, and whoever wants to be first among
you must be your slave.*

(Matt. 20:25–27)

• • •

Imitate me, as I also imitate Christ.

(1 Cor. 11:1)

• • •

*And He personally gave some to be apostles, some
prophets, some evangelists, some pastors and
teachers, for the training of the saints in the work of
ministry, to build up the body of Christ.*

(Eph. 4:11–12)

• • •

*Do what you have learned and received and heard
and seen in me, and the God of peace will be with you.*

(Phil. 4:9)

10
Leaders

The key to successful leadership today is influence,
not authority.

—Ken Blanchard

SEVERAL MONTHS AGO I (Michael) had the chance to travel to Dublin, Ireland, a city rich in history, architecture, and culture. But, as anyone who has ever traveled internationally knows, also a city that is a long way away from Nashville, Tennessee. One of the keys to making a trip like that work is the speed at which you get rid of the jet lag. Because overseas flights from the U.S. often begin in the afternoon or evening but arrive at the destination in the morning, the temptation is to go immediately to the hotel and go to sleep. After all, your body thinks it's 2:00 a.m. even though the clock says it's 8:00 a.m. the next morning.

Do not do this.

Let me repeat: Do not do this. A much wiser course of action is to embrace the fatigue and stay up and moving until it's bedtime according to the local clock. No doubt the day is going to be miserable, but your body will adjust to the new time much more quickly. Better one day of miserable tiredness than a ruined trip.

So arriving in Dublin at 8:00 a.m. local time, I set about trying to explore a foreign city. There were buildings I assumed were important on every corner. Streets that must have been hundreds of years old. And churches that have stood the test of time. Now maybe it was the jet lag talking, but none of it interested me very much. I wandered the streets of Dublin for hours in boredom, eventually getting lost trying to find my way back to the hotel. Finally, at 9:30 p.m. I thought it was acceptable to go to bed, and after sleeping for eleven hours, I woke up and everything was different.

I spent the next morning walking the same streets and seeing the same things. It was the same environment that had bored me to tears the day before, but with one key difference: I had a guide. A tour guide to be exact. And for several hours we went on a walking tour of downtown Dublin, learning wonderful bits of history and incredible stories of political intrigue and societal change. Riveting, not boring. Arresting, not mundane. Amazing what a guide can do.

> *Amazing what a guide can do.*

Up to this point, we've seen the role truth plays in transformational discipleship. We've also seen that discipleship is most transformational when a person is in a vulnerable posture. The final ingredient, though, is leadership. We need people who can rightly apply the truth to others in a vulnerable posture. Without that leadership, would-be disciples are just wandering around aimlessly, waiting for one day to turn into the next.

The Intersection of Truth and Vulnerability

Something amazing happens when leaders embrace their responsibility to help people apply the truth of God's Word to those in a vulnerable position. It's uniquely powerful not only because of the living and active nature of Scripture but also because people in such a posture are uniquely moldable and teachable. They are uniquely open to the move of God, ready to embrace His truth as never before.

As we've said, sometimes that posture of vulnerability happens by our choice. We intentionally position ourselves so God can work in us through a variety of means. But more often vulnerability comes as a result of often painful or difficult circumstances in life. Such circumstances can leave anyone floundering, looking for direction and guidance in a life that has suddenly been turned upside down.

When life gets flipped upside down, we lose our equilibrium. Normal is gone. Uncertainty and doubt begin to creep in. In a position like that, believers are searching for understanding and meaning. They ask questions. They examine the foundation their lives are built on. They search and seek, and one of two things can easily happen during a time when people are vulnerable.

People can give up during times like that. They can abandon what they once believed, convinced that they were wrong about God and His plan for the universe. But in as much as people might leave, there is also an incredible opportunity for life transformation to happen during this time. And God has often chosen to use leaders as His agents during times like these.

Think about how Paul described spiritual maturity to the church at Ephesus:

> Then we will no longer be little children, tossed by the waves and blown around be every wind of teaching, by human cunning with cleverness in the techniques of deceit. (Eph. 4:14)

It's a great description of a disciple. Someone who knows the difference between truth and falsehood. Someone whose roots are deep enough not to be tossed about by the wind and waves. Steady, calm, persevering—these are marks of those who are growing in Christ. But notice that this description of mature faith, of those who are growing up into Christ (v. 15), is linked to the gift of leaders Jesus has given to the church:

> And He personally gave some to be apostles, some prophets, some evangelists, some pastors and teachers, for the training of the saints in the work of the ministry, to build up the body of Christ, until we all reach unity in the faith and in the knowledge of God's Son, growing into a mature man with a statue measured by Christ's fullness. (Eph. 4:11–13)

When deep, life-changing situations happen, leaders can help their people regain their stability. They can help them find equilibrium. The way they do that is by helping people view their lives, both the good and bad things in them, through lenses that conform to biblical truth.

> **When deep, life-changing situations happen, leaders can help their people regain their stability.**

Everyone views life in a certain way. Their perspective is formed by many things—upbringing, economics, race, experience . . . and faith. All those factors together form a kind of lens people wear, and everything they observe is filtered through those lenses. During times of difficulty, people start evaluating their lenses. They wonder if they're constructed of the right stuff or if perhaps they're faulty. When leaders are active in the lives of their people, they can help people have the right kind of lenses in order to process everything coming their way.

In this way leaders become the kind of guide for their people that can keep them from wandering around aimlessly. Much like Michael's tour guide in Dublin, a leader can point to circumstances and apply biblical truth, helping people see in a whole new way. They can help people find meaning and direction as they together go through the constant process of making sure our lenses are made from the right stuff. Given that as the goal for leaders, to help people have the right lenses in which to view the world, there are a couple of cautions good for leaders to remember.

Beware the Information

Leaders should be careful not to become Pez dispensers of information. A Pez dispenser is pretty easy to operate. Someone wants a piece of candy, so they take the Pez dispenser, tilt back the character's

> *Leaders should be careful not to become Pez dispensers of information.*

head, and out comes a sugary treat. Many leaders functionally lead the same way.

They see themselves primarily as the theological, relational, or ecclesiological expert—the one with all the answers. People come to them asking questions, and these leaders simply tilt their head back and dispense information in a palatable way, congratulating themselves afterward for actually knowing the answer to the question someone was asking.

Of course, information is important. But we must realize that rarely are people asking questions simply for the sake of information. Theological questions are often personal questions in disguise.

People pose questions about theology, the nature of good and evil, and about suffering and sovereignty. On the surface a question might sound like an innocent search for knowledge. Often, though, something lies behind the question. Something personal or painful is driving it. If leaders are too quick simply to answer the question, the person asking it is not well served. Sure, the information might be right, but a leader who only answers fails to take advantage of the redemptive conversation that might follow. There is no better example to follow in this than Jesus.

Have you ever noticed the frustrating way Jesus often answered questions? Sometimes it was with another question. Sometimes it was with a seemingly unrelated parable or teaching. Rarely, though, is it with plain and simple information.

> *Often, though, something lies behind the question.*

Why did Jesus do this? Was it to make people mad? Was it because He enjoyed seeing them roll their eyes? Or was some divine intentionality going on here?

Perhaps Jesus was interested in transformation more than information.

Sure, it would have been exponentially faster to score discipleship in the same manner we do a spelling bee. Just simply dispense the information, have them memorize it by rote, and regurgitate it on cue. People might have considered Him to be more of an expert at the time. They might have lauded His incredible capacity for recalling information and His brilliant insight more than they did. But these things seemed to matter little to Jesus. He understood the fact that people's theological questions come from somewhere, that people are looking for the right lenses through which to view the world. But those lenses aren't constructed through an information dump. That information must be applied at the right time and in the right situation, and Jesus refused to settle for anything less. Neither should we. We must press further than information regardless of how messy it becomes or how long it takes.

If we settle for only dispensing information, not only will change in people's lives fall short of transformation, but we will begin to lead people down a dangerous path. Slowly but surely people will begin to define their discipleship exclusively in terms of intellect. That is, if you know the right answers, you are following Jesus more and more closely.

That's not to lessen the need for good informational content. That's one of the core tasks of leaders. Indeed, that's the defining characteristic for Paul that separated the leaders of the church—the "overseers"—from the "deacons." If you compare the list of qualifications Paul listed for both groups found in 1 Timothy 3:1–13, the difference in those two lists comes back to being an "able teacher" (1 Tim. 3:2). But there is a great amount of distance between the head and the heart.

There once was a group of people who were proficient in knowledge. They could recite the law and prophets at length and were considered by the people of their day to be religious experts. And yet on the inside their hearts were made of stone. They were the Pharisees, and we all know how Jesus spoke to them.

Practically, church leaders know this to be true as well. Think about those in your own congregation that truly follow Jesus. Those that walk closely with Him. Those that live in a vulnerable posture and are ready to hear, accept, and obey the truth. They might be proficient in knowledge, but then again, they might have no formal education. They might not be able to wax eloquently about systematic theology. That leads us to understand the danger in equating discipleship too closely with intellectual knowledge but also to see that a component of discipleship is often neglected: Love.

Lead Because You Love

What does the greatest command hinge upon? Love. What will never pass away, even after faith and hope are gone? Love. What will be the defining characteristic of followers of Jesus? Love.

Love is the mark of the disciple. But here's the problem: You can't teach love.

You can teach how to memorize Scripture, everything from acrostic memory devices to methods of placing cards for reading at strategic places. Similarly, you can teach someone how to fast—what to expect on day 1, 2, and so forth, and how to respond to the temptation of hunger. You can teach someone how to pray. The tools abound in terms of journals, philosophies, and books. But how do you teach someone to love?

This is perhaps the one element of discipleship that can't be faked. Surely there are many, according to Jesus, who might perform miracles, drive out demons, and do all other kinds of religious things that will not enter the kingdom of heaven. We can become adept at "playing disciple" by our sheer acts of will. We can even force ourselves into positions of service and postures of generosity. But love? Real genuine love? That's something you can't manufacture.

Nevertheless, Jesus said, "All people will know that you are My disciples, if you have love for one another" (John 13:35). Despite this statement all our current metrics of discipleship focus on things like knowledge of the Bible and time spent in prayer. Those are all also important marks of discipleship, but love is infinitely more difficult (and perhaps impossible) to quantify. Yet leaders are called to be the vanguards of love for those that follow them. To lead well, you must love naturally. As Jesus did.

Nobody ever loved by gritting their teeth and deciding to do it. It's not like that. True, love is grown over time, and like most other things, our appetite for love grows through exercises of the will. That is, we choose to engage in activities of love even when we don't feel like it because we believe that in doing so, our love will grow. But ultimately, even these actions can't force us to love.

> **To lead well, you must love naturally.**

That's actually why love is the defining characteristic of discipleship—because love—true love—can only come from a true, vibrant, and constant experience of the gospel. The gospel is what love is—that's the true measure of love. Those who truly love demonstrate they have been loved and are growing in their understanding of the great love of God in Christ.

Leaders must decide to press love to the forefront rather than information. Information must still be learned. Truth must be encountered and the right lenses put in place, but love must lead the believers there first. So be careful, leaders, that we don't treat intellect as the measure of following Jesus. Information dispensation is the easier way, but Jesus wants us to take the harder—and longer—way to discipleship.

The Long Way

That's the second caution for leaders desiring to help people along in transformational discipleship—strap in because it's going to take a long time. This makes the process of making disciples immensely more messy and frustrating than we would like. We live in a Twitter culture where everything is boiled down to 140 characters. If something takes too long, we look for a different way. If the Internet takes too long to load, we try to find another network. If the dinner we ordered takes too long to be served, we ask to speak to a manager. If the book is getting boring, we look for the Cliffs Notes or skip to the last page. We hate the long way at any time and in any situation because we have been conditioned by our culture to expect instantaneous, immediate gratification.

God has a different agenda. In His mind the long way isn't the wrong way. And the reason the long way isn't the wrong way is because God is more committed to who we're becoming than where we're going. This is a significant adjustment for us to make because we have in our minds a picture of a "mature disciple," and we can become so fixated on a person meeting certain qualifications, developing certain habits, and practicing certain principles that we can lose sight of the goal of inner transformation. We must come to love and accept the long road if we want to be engaged in transformational discipleship.

> *We must come to love and accept the long road if we want to be engaged in transformational discipleship.*

In Exodus 13 we find the children of Israel living out the deliverance of God. Under Moses' leadership, God has miraculously and powerfully brought His people out of four hundred years of slavery. Not only has He brought them out, but their captors sent them on their way with gifts. He has brought them out under the same banner that He promised Abraham centuries earlier—to make them a great nation and give them a land of their own. That's the destination—the promised land. But then something curious happens:

> When Pharaoh let the people go, God did not lead them along the road to the land of the Philistines, even though it was nearby; for God said, "The people will change their minds and return to Egypt if they face war." So He led the people around toward the Red Sea along the road of the wilderness. And the Israelites left the land of Egypt in battle formation. (Exod. 13:17–18)

It's interesting because of where they were headed. They were headed to the promised land, but God didn't take them on a straight line. He instead led them in a far longer route, which clues us in that perhaps the Lord isn't only interested in just getting His people to the promised land after all. Maybe He's got some ulterior motives in their deliverance.

Now this shouldn't come as a surprise to us or to them because we see this same attitude displayed by God during the awful plagues He brought on the Egyptians. Remember those? Gnats. Frogs. Blood. Darkness. Grasshoppers. Boils. And then finally, the death of the firstborn son of every creature save those who were protected by the blood on the doorpost. Now here's the question: If God were only interested in getting His people out of Egypt, wouldn't it have been far faster and easier just to skip to the worst plague to begin with? Why go through all nine before getting to the last one?

The answer again is because the long way isn't the wrong way. God wasn't only interested in getting the people out; He was also interested in demonstrating something about Himself. If you look back at each one of the plagues, each one of them corresponds to a different god in the Egyptian belief system. The Egyptians worshipped the Nile. God turns the Nile to blood. The Egyptians worshipped the sun. God brought about darkness. You see it? God is systematically demonstrating His dominance over every god in the Egyptians' minds and hearts, proving His absolute dominance and power. So God's interest was not just getting the people out; He also wanted to show every onlooker that the only true God was the God of Israel.

Now it's one thing to say that. Perhaps even some of the Israelites knew that. But it's another thing to find yourself in the place where the Israelites now found themselves. Just imagine it for a second. As we proceed through chapter 14, we find that Pharaoh changes his mind and mounts an incredible posse to go and bring back the slaves. So there you are. An Israelite freshly freed from bondage. You march out of Egypt with a song in your heart, laughing at this turn of events. You think to yourself: *Should we really be going this way? I mean, nothing can stop us now. Let's make a beeline for the promised land.* But you push those doubts away. Moses is leading you, and he's proven to be worth following so far, right?

But your hesitation starts to grow as you keep following. You look around the terrain and think that it looks like he's leading you in circles. You go a bit one way, then another way—like maybe this guy doesn't really know where he's going. Then your doubt reaches a fevered pitch when you find yourself confronted with an enormous body of water. No way across. And you camp. Then, as if it couldn't get any worse, the ground literally starts to shake. It feels like a mighty thunderstorm or an earthquake, and you turn to see your worst nightmare coming true. Thousands upon thousands of chariots and soldiers swarming down upon you. The sea is in front of you; the army is at your back. And utter and complete panic sets in.

I wonder if, in the midst of the tears and the screaming for mercy, there was a moment when some reflective Israelite had the presence of mind to think: *Why? Why oh why did we come this way? I knew we should have gone a different way, but now Moses or God or whoever has led us into a trap with no way out.*

As leaders we might ask the same kind of questions. Why are these people so obstinate? Why do they continue to sin, over and over again? Why isn't anyone reading the Bible? Why am I teaching the same thing over and over again, and yet people's lives seem to be unchanged? Why? Why did we come this way? Why didn't God just take me into the promised land? That place where everything goes like I think it should? Why isn't my church experiencing the revival? Why are people taking such small steps on the road to maturity? Why did we come this way, when the other way would have been so much shorter?

One basic answer to those questions we see from the passage is this: God knows us better than we know ourselves.

Look back at verse 18. The Israelites marched out of captivity in battle formation. Now here's the thing: This was no army. They were brick makers. Not one person among them had been schooled in combat.

> **God knows us better than we know ourselves.**

You might think of it like this. Let's say you are part of the football team at your school, and it's a great football team. So good, in fact, that you have no hope of making the team. Nevertheless, the coach agrees to put you on the team though all you do at practice is show up and sit on the sidelines. You don't dress for the games. You don't ever put on pads. You don't even hold the water bottles. But the team you're on wins the state championship, and you get a championship ring. Now imagine walking down the hallway of your school not only wearing that ring but boasting about it. Talking about your pivotal role in the victory. Doesn't make sense, right?

In a similar way the Israelites had done absolutely nothing to deliver themselves from Egypt. They didn't fight one battle, lift one sword, or make one triumph. Yet when they walked out of Egypt, they walked out like they were the Roman legion. But God knew them better than they knew themselves. Though they were confident, we read in verse 17 that God led them the long way because if they faced war they would change their minds and return to Egypt.

To put it simply, they were not yet ready. They needed the long way, whether they recognized it or not. This might be true not only of those we are leading but even of ourselves. We think we're ready. We're in battle formation. We're ready to see the work and power of God manifested through us. We're ready—at least in our minds. But God knows us better than we know ourselves. He knows how we struggle with pride. He understands how quickly we might turn from Him. And He knows that lifting us too quickly will lose us.

So He takes us the long way. And that's not the wrong way. Because a funny thing happens on the long way—you actually do become something rather than just go somewhere. In fact, you might say it like this: the most formative parts of your lives—the ones that fashion real character and dependence and faith and perseverance—are often the most difficult. When you feel like you are wandering around in circles, when you don't seem to be making any progress, and when you might even feel trapped—those are the forging times. The book of James says it like this: "Consider it a great joy, my brothers [and sisters], whenever you experience various trials, knowing that the testing of your faith produces endurance. But endurance must do its complete work, so that you may be mature and complete, lacking nothing" (James 1:2–4).

Though the long way might seem like wasted time from our perspective, God isn't in the business of wasting time. With God nothing is ever wasted. Every experience is not just about the experience itself but about the building and shaping and preparing of the person going through the experience.

> **With God nothing is ever wasted.**

The long way isn't the wrong way. When we find ourselves on the long way, we can choose to be frustrated at the length. We can choose to doubt because of the sea in front of us. We can choose to quake in terror at the army approaching behind. Or we can choose to believe in a God who is interested in not just getting us to a destination but forming us into a people. Embrace the long way, leaders. Love the long way because it's on the long road that people don't just behave differently; they become different.

The Necessity of Leadership

Because the road is so long, we need leaders who are willing to walk alongside us. We need people who, when the going actually does get tough, to apply biblical truth so we can view the world and our lives through the right set of lenses. But the last piece of transformational discipleship brings us full circle because leadership is not only necessary to transformational discipleship; it's also the end result of transformational discipleship. As Alexander Acosta told us, "In creating disciples, we are creating leaders."

It's instructive to remember that the command of Jesus wasn't to make converts. Nor was it to make church members. It was to make disciples—transformed followers who embrace the same commission that led to their own transformation.

C. S. Lewis wrote, "Rabbits beget rabbits; horses beget horses; humans beget humans, not statues or portraits."[1] We reproduce our own kind, our own nature. Nobody goes to the delivery room of a hospital expecting to bring a dolphin home, because we all reproduce according to our own nature.

When we are commanded to make disciples, it is assumed that we are disciples ourselves. We are, therefore, "begetting" our own kind. We are doing so in order that those disciples might make other disciples who might in turn make other disciples and so on. It's multiplication versus addition, and it's the way Jesus told us to operate. Victor Vellanueva from Yucatan Independent University in Mexico described it this way: "I call this the law of transfer of life because we transfer, we transmit, what we have learned, so in turn people can do it with others."

> *It's multiplication versus addition, and it's the way Jesus told us to operate.*

Leaders must recognize that their success is measured not in the number of followers they gather but in the number of leaders they unleash into God's mission. Unfortunately, though, this often remains in the realm of theory—something we know we should be doing but rarely participate in. But moving people into such relationships and positions is much simpler than we want to make it.

The best way to move people into leadership is to move them into leadership.

Just do it. Even if they don't know everything. Even if they aren't perfect. Even if they might not be entirely ready. Just do it.

Expect it. And then take that opportunity as yet another opportunity to help truth intersect with these people because they will, no doubt, be in a posture of vulnerability.

Many times the best way of learning is to be doing.

Earlier in the book you learned about Steve Murrell and the church he planted in Manilla, Victory Church. When I (Philip) talked with Steve, he had a fascinating perspective on leadership. The growth of their church by his own description had been out of control. It had seemingly always been that way. But in discussing it with him, it was as much by choice as by accident or happenstance. Steve described that making disciples occurred through the context of relationships in which one believer brought several friends to worship and engaged them in a Bible study. It is a standard Bible study all members attend, and it is their "starting point" for beginning small groups. Once people made a faith decision to become a Christian, they had already experienced all that was necessary to lead a new Bible study group.

Now for many of us in the United States, this may seem rushing a bit. But for Victory Church, the goal is to produce as many disciples as possible through as many groups as possible. To do so, they need as many leaders as possible. Therefore, every new believer is viewed as a new leader. As soon as they are converted and finish the initial four-week Bible study, they are essentially commissioned to start a new group. It is a church that believes in producing a new generation of believers . . . every day.

A healthy leader understands the necessity of creating more and more leaders and takes an active role in doing so. When we are willing to do this, it's because truth is intersecting with us, too. We are not insecure about others leading because we are daily reminding ourselves of the gospel and our new identity in Christ. We are prepared to help others take on responsibility because we are daily disciplining ourselves to be praying, fasting, studying, and all the rest. We are seeing that leadership isn't only necessary to the process of discipleship; it's also the result of discipleship.

Ironically, these principles are just as applicable to leaders as they are to those we are trying to empower to be leaders. We, too, learn best by doing. So get started. Engage with people on the long road of discipleship. And love what God is doing in and through you.

11
A Transformed Disciple

IN THE LEADER'S FINAL hours, He was almost completely alone. He faced death without the company of those who swore their allegiance. Most of His trusted and closest friends deserted Him. Some fled and painfully betrayed Him. The world scorned Him.

But not this disciple.

This disciple would remain faithful. His mind was fully committed, his will set on his Leader's agenda, and his heart thrilled by the intimacy of the relationship with his Teacher. He was in awe of his King, humbled to be included in the inner circle. This disciple wrote of the greatness of his Leader's life:

> And there are also many other things that Jesus did,
> which, if they were written one by one, I suppose not
> even the world itself could contain the books that would
> be written. (John 21:25)

He was Jesus' disciple, and he was transformed. His name was John.

John followed Jesus to the cross when all others abandoned Him. While Jesus was dying on the cross, He entrusted His mother to John (John 19:26). Jesus entrusted the vision of eternity to John, the book of Revelation that uncovers the future. John was a pillar in the movement of the Christian faith, and God used him to significantly impact the church. He wrote five of the books in the New Testament.

With all that happened in John's life, his greatest source of satisfaction and identity was that God loved him. In the Gospel account he wrote about Jesus, and he simply referred to himself as "the one Jesus loved" (John 20:2).

The one Jesus loved.

Overwhelmed

Disciples who are transformed are still overwhelmed with the truth of God's love; they are continually in awe that Jesus loves them. Transformation is stalled when we grow calloused to His love by moving out of a vulnerable posture and into a position of self-dependence.

> *Transformation is stalled when we grow calloused to His love.*

When God's love transforms the heart of a disciple, obedience follows. The love of God transformed John's heart and caused him to love God and others. His reliance on God's love resulted in transformed living. Notice how John's deep appreciation for God's love impacted every facet of his life.

Love drove John to understand that God had initiated the relationship.

Love consists in this: not that we loved God, but that He loved us and sent His Son to be the propitiation for our sins. Dear friends, if God loved us in this way, we also must love one another. (1 John 4:10–11)

The loving sacrifice by Jesus led John to prioritize relationships.

This is how we have come to know love: He laid down His life for us. We should also lay down our lives for our brothers. If anyone has this world's goods and sees his brother in need but closes his eyes to his need how can God's love reside in him? (1 John 3:16–17)

John walked away from the idols of the world and focused on the One who is eternal.

Do not love the world or the things that belong to the world. If anyone loves the world, love for the Father is not in him. For everything that belongs to the world— the lust of the flesh, the lust of the eyes, and the pride in one's lifestyle—is not from the Father, but is from the world. (1 John 2:15–16)

John learned to demonstrate his love for God with a joyous obedience.

This is how we know that we love God's children when we love God and obey His commands. For this is what love for God is: to keep His commands. Now His commands are not a burden. (1 John 5:2–3)

The interviews our TD research held with the experts in the field of discipleship ran the gamut of settings, styles, and situations. However, one common factor in all of them was passion. The love we see displayed and taught by Christ was evident in the lives of these men and women. On several occasions our team would come home with the story that the person being interviewed was "coming out of their chair they were so excited" or "brought to tears because of their love for the church."

One such passionate person was Robertson McQuilkin. He has been leading in the field of discipleship for many years. He has experienced much of God's ministry as a missionary in Japan. He has also led many to be leaders in the church as the president of a Christian university. And he has experienced great grief in the loss of his wife to Alzheimer's disease. But through it all, he has always desired to grow deeper in his walk with Christ. During the interview with him, he said these words:

> The more I know Him, the more I love Him. The more I love Him, the more I obey Him. The more I obey Him, the more I become like Him. The more I become like Him, the better I know Him. The better I know Him, I love Him the more. And the more I love Him, I reach a new level of likeness to Him.

It is this kind of spirit the church needs more of today. The passion for God's love to take hold of our lives and change everything. Everything,

The Sweet Spot

Our hope for you is that you will lead others to be in the Transformational Sweet Spot. The convergence of truth, posture, and leaders can bring about change in the lives of people around you. To get them there, we encourage you to be proactive. Discipleship is constantly happening in people's lives. They are growing in their knowledge about work, loyalty to their favorite team, and investing in what matters most to them at the moment. To lead them in transformational discipleship will take special effort on your part.

First, spend time with God by studying His Word and being a person of prayer. In *Transformational Church*, our friends Thom Rainer and Ed Stetzer wrote about how trust in God's Word and confidence in prayer are vital to the growth of a church. The same is obviously true for all individual believers—even leaders like you. Ask the Holy Spirit to show you what needs to be done next in the discipling ministry of your church, and do so with the mind-set that obedience is your only option.

> Ask the Holy Spirit to show you what needs to be done next in the discipling ministry of your church.

Next, find a way to help those in the church assess their own discipleship journey. As stated earlier, identity is a huge factor in a transformational journey. But we find that people are painfully unaware of who they are, where they are, or what is supposed to be occurring in discipleship. Out of the TD research that led us to many of the principles you read about here, a Transformational Discipleship Assessment has been compiled. Just go to www.LifeWay.com/TDA to find out more.[1]

Now we realize that many people may think that an assessment, test, or inventory may appear unspiritual in light of the lofty goals of discipleship. However, as pastors, we believe in helping them know where they are weak and where they are strong. An objective tool can help with that journey.

Get a plan together. In an accompanying DVD study, the three of us will teach about implementing the principles you've read about in this book. The Transformational Sweet Spot should be the normative place for disciples, but it is not where we find many people. In order to get them there, a leader needs to apply the truth to people who have put themselves in the right posture. You are the leader to help put that strategy together and invite people into the middle of it.

Finally, talk about discipleship with your church. A lot. When we advocate this, we do not mean just announce that you are holding classes on a particular night. Instead, teach, preach, discuss, and have private conversations about transformation. It is God's intention for His people to grow. The church needs to know that if it is a priority for God, then it is a priority for the leaders in the church.

> **You are the leader to help put that strategy together.**

In one of the churches I (Philip) led, my favorite time of the week was Thursday nights. At that time a group of six guys got together with me at a local coffee shop. I always had an agenda. We always studied the truth. And we always applied it to our lives—including me. But to do so, as the leader, I had to verbalize truth and question the guys about its application. At the end of my life, I have no doubt that those friendly, challenging, laughter-filled, coffee shop conversations will be among the most fruitful times of ministry.

So decide right now, when and how you are going to start talking about discipleship. We must be intentional for discipleship to be transformational. If you don't believe that, just take a quick assessment of what haphazard methods and occasional emphasis has done for discipling people so far. God has given you the greatest resources possible: salvation, His Spirit, the Word, and the church. It is time to take them on the journey that will change

> **It is God's intention for His people to grow.**

how they view God's kingdom and all of life. But do so with the right heart.

God's love is transformational. When a disciple encounters the truth of God's love while in a vulnerable posture, he will be continually changed.

Allow God's love to transform your heart.

And be the leader who applies God's truth to the hearts of others.

About the Authors

Eric Geiger serves as the Vice President of the Church Resource Division at LifeWay Christian Resources. Eric received his doctorate in leadership and church ministry from Southern Seminary. Eric has served local churches, most recently investing eight years as an executive and teaching pastor of Christ Fellowship Miami. He has authored or coauthored several books including the best selling church leadership book, *Simple Church*. Eric is married to Kaye, and they have two daughters: Eden and Evie. During his free time, Eric enjoys dating his wife, playing with his daughters, and shooting basketball.

Michael Kelley is the Director of Discipleship for Lifeway Christian Resources. His previous works include *Holy Vocabulary, The Tough Sayings of Jesus,* and *Wednesdays Were Pretty Normal: A Boy, Cancer and God.* He holds a Master of Divinity degree from Beeson Divinity School in Birmingham, Alabama. Michael and his wife have three children and live in Nashville, Tennessee.

Philip Nation is the Director of Ministry Development for LifeWay Research. He received his doctor of ministry in missional leadership from Southeastern Seminary. Philip has served as a pastor and church planter. His other works include *Compelled: Living the Mission of God* and serving as general editor of *The Mission of God Study Bible*. Philip and his wife Angie have two sons, Andrew and Chris.

NOTES

Chapter One: Deficient Discipleship

1. Dietrich Bonhoeffer, *The Cost of Discipleship* (New York: Touchstone, 1995), 59.
2. *The Early Goebbels Diaries*, entries for November 6 and 23, 1925.
3. Der Angriff. Aufsätze aus der Kampfzeit by Joseph Goebbels (newspaper).
4. A. W. Tozer, *I Call It Heresy* (Rockville, MD: Wildside, 2010), 13.
5. Bonhoeffer, *The Cost of Discipleship*, 44–45.

Chapter Two: Disciple to Win

1. The concept of offensive versus defensive discipleship is adapted from the teaching on the difference between offensive and defensive parenting in the great book, *Gospel Powered Parenting* by William P. Farley.
2. Martin Luther wrote this in his *Prayer Book of the Psalms*.
3. From Søren Kierkegaard's work on "sickness unto death."

Chapter Three: Transformational Sweet Spot

1. Quote by Scottish pastor Thomas Chalmers.
2. John Calvin, *Institutes of the Christian Religion*, vol. 1, John T. McNeil, ed., Ford Lewis Battles, trans. (Louisville: Westminster John Knox Press, 1960), 108.

3. Fyodor Dostoyevsky, *The Brothers Karamazov* (New York: Random House, 1996 Modern Library Edition), 58.
4. G. K. Beale, *We Become What We Worship: A Biblical Theology of Idolatry* (Downers Grove, IL: InterVarsity Press, 2008), 16.
5. Augustine, *Confessions*, Book 6, Chapter viii.
6. Augustine, *Confessions*, IV.vi.9.
7. C. S. Lewis, *Mere Christianity* (New York: HarperOne, 1952), 50.
8. Blaise Pascal, "Morality and Doctrine," *Thoughts* (New York: Collier & Sons, 1910), 138.
9. Kenneth Boa, *Conformed to His Image: Biblical and Practical Approached to Spiritual Formation* (Grand Rapids: Zondervan, 2001). This is one of the best books of all time on spiritual formation/discipleship. Much of this section comes from learning through this book.
10. Speech given by Winston Churchill in the House of Commons on May 17, 1916.

Chapter Four: The Gospel Lens

1. C. J. Mahaney, *The Cross Centered Life* (Colorado Springs, CO: Multnomah, 2002), 132.
2. Matt Chandler in Trevin Wax's *Counterfeit Gospels: Rediscovering the Good News in a World of False Hope* (Chicago: Moody Publishers, 2011).
3. Jonathan Edwards, "God's Chief End in Creation," *The Works of Jonathan Edwards* (London: William Bell, 1834), 98.
4. John Dillenberger, ed. *Martin Luther: Selections from His Writings* Garden City, NY: Doubleday, 1961), 11–12.
5. Martin Luther, *History of the Reformation of the Sixteenth Century*, vol. 2, Jean Henri Merle, ed., H. White, trans. (New York: R. Carter & Brothers, 1847), 138.
6. Kyle tells the story in his book, *One Red Paperclip*. After all, he does need to fill the house with furniture.
7. William Temple said this epic statement. "This We Believe: Eight Truths Presbyterians Affirm" by Stephen Plunkett (2002), 93.

8. Charles Spurgeon, *Treasury of David* (Grand Rapids: Kregel Publications, 1976).

9. Timothy Keller, *The Centrality of the Gospel*. A White paper found at: www.redeemer2.com/resources/papers/centrality. pdf. Keller is the founding pastor of Redeemer Presbyterian Church in New York City and has been influential in helping the church understand that "the gospel is not merely the ABC's of the Christian faith, but the A-Z." We believe anything he writes is a must read.

Chapter Six: The Discipline Lens

1. Adorniam Judson Gordon, *The Found the Street: 20 Transformed Lives That Reveal a Touch of Eternity*, V. Raymond Edman, ed. (Grand Rapids: Zondervan, 1960), 77.

2. Charles Spurgeon, *Prayer and Spiritual Warfare* (New Kingsington, PA: Whitaker House, 1998), 122.

3. See Edward M. Plass, comp., *What Luther Says*, vol. 1 (St. Louis: Condordia Publishing House, 1997), 234–35.

Chapter Seven: Weakness

1. Viktor E. Frankl, *Man's Search for Ultimate Meaning* (Cambridge: Perseus Books, 1975), 133.

2. Philip Yancey's thinking on Job's suffering as presented in *The Bible Jesus Read* resonated with us (Grand Rapids: Zondervan, 2007).

3. James Montgomery Boice, *Romans*, 4 vol. (Grand Rapids: Baker, 2005).

4. The quote comes from Brandon Skjoldal-Blackwood, one of the pastors Eric served alongside in Miami.

5. "Center Aisle" song by Caedmon's Call (Word Entertainment, 1997).

Chapter Eight: Interdependent

1. Deitrich Bonhoeffer, *Life Together* (New York: Harper & Row, 1954), 112.

2. Ibid., 77.

3. D. A. Carson, *Love in Hard Places* (Wheaton, IL: Crossway, 2002), 61.

4. Matt Chandler, *Philippians Study Guide: To Live Is Christ and to Die Is Gain* (The Hub, 2009). See www.christianbook.com/philippians-study-guide-live-christ-gain/matt-chander.

Chapter Nine: Outward

1. C. H. Spurgeon, "A Sermon and a Reminiscence." A short sermon from the "Sword and Trowel" (March 1873).

Chapter Ten: Leaders

1. C. S. Lewis, *Mere Christianity* (New York: HarperOne, 1952), chapter 23.

Chapter Eleven: A Transformed Disciple

1. You can find out more about the Transformational Discipleship Assessment by going to www.LifeWay.com/TDA.

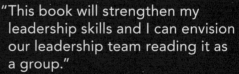

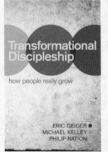